Much of Iran's cuisine is essentially vegeta
Although kababs are popular restaurant f
represent only a small sampling of the dishes
eat at home. Persian cooking, with its emphasis on
fresh, natural ingredients corresponds with the trend
in eating that's spreading across America. "Join the
delicious revolution!" as Alice Waters says; "Eat simply,
eat together, eat seasonally, shop at farmers markets."

The recipes in this book—each accompanied by
a photograph of the finished dish—come straight
from Najmieh's kitchen and include not only the
classics of Persian cooking, but also some soon-to-be
favorites, such as quinoa or kale cooked Persian-style.
You'll discover delicious side dishes, from cooling,
yogurt-based salads and tasty dips and spreads, to
more sustaining platters of grains, beans and fresh
herbs; tasty "kukus"—frittata-style omelets filled with
vegetables and herbs; spice-infused fish; mouth-
watering meatballs and kababs served on flat breads
with tangy sauces; every kind of rice—including the
incomparable polow topped with various sweet and
sour braises; not to mention, delightfully aromatic
cakes and cookies to round off meals or enjoy as a
snack in between.

So, jump in and explore. You will find inspiration
as well as practical guidance: a great age-old
cuisine presented for today's world.

JOON

PERSIAN COOKING
MADE SIMPLE

NAJMIEH BATMANGLIJ

MAGE PUBLISHERS
WASHINGTON DC

Editorial Direction: Zal Batmanglij
Art Direction: Rostam Batmanglij

Photos were styled by Najmieh and shot by Mohammad Batmanglij, except as noted for the pages below:

Nader Souri: 13, 16, 17, 22, 23, 30, 31, 33
Afshin Bakhtiar: 6, 24, 26, 87, 94, 124, 134
Amir Naderi: 29
Maryam Zandi: 28

Library of Congress Cataloging-in-Publication Data
Names: Batmanglij, Najmieh, author.
Title: Joon : Persian cooking made simple / Najmieh Batmanglij.
Description: First edition. | Washington DC : Mage Publishers, 2016. | Includes index.
Identifiers: LCCN 2016019020| ISBN 1933823720 (hardcover : alk. paper) | ISBN 9781933823836 (ebook)
Subjects: LCSH: Cooking, Iranian. | LCGFT: Cookbooks.
Classification: LCC TX725.I7 B368 2016 | DDC 641.5955–dc23
LC record available at https://lccn.loc.gov/2016019020

First edition
ISBN 13: 978-1-933823-72-0
4th printing

eBook ISBN: 978-1-933823-83-6

Manufactured in Korea

Visit Mage online at www.mage.com • as@mage.com

For my sons Zal and Rostam,
and for their generation.

C O N T

E N T S

Najmieh at the Fresh
Farms Market in Dupont
Circle, Washington DC.

INTRODUCTION

I was inspired to write this book by my sons and their friends, a generation eager to explore the pleasures of cooking, as well as looking for guidance on how to prepare healthy and delicious dishes in a way that fits with their busy lives. ✑ With this in mind, I have concentrated on two main things: to simplify the cooking of my favorite Persian recipes—many of them vegetarian, and now also "one pot" dishes; and to reduce the cooking time. Many of the recipes in this book will take an hour or less. ✑ Before you start cooking, do read the introductory section about essential ingredients for a basic Persian pantry (pages 10–37). I have tried to keep them simple. You'll find information about herbs and spices, and how to use them for best results. Be sure to also read "Preparing to Cook" on page 39, where I strongly recommend that you use the organizing system known as *mise en place* (from the French "put in place") as it will really help you in the kitchen. ✑ Like the 13th-century Persian poet Rumi, I consider the kitchen a metaphor for life: cooking at home not only nourishes your body but also helps you gain discipline and confidence in everything else that you do. Use this book to cook together, to eat together, to tell good stories to each other, and to be creative. ✑ As Iranians say, *Nush-e joon!*—a traditional Persian wish that a meal will be enjoyed.

pomegranate

walnuts

baby almonds

unripe grapes

raisins

lime

sesame seeds

unripe greengages

pistachios

Persian cucumber

zest of orange

Persian shallots

dried Persian lime

basmati rice

fava beans

rose petals

sumac

orange blossom water

barberries

rose water

kashk (dried buttermilk)

saffron threads

Italian eggplant

Chinese eggplant

pomegranate molasses

grape molasses

THE ESSENTIAL PERSIAN PANTRY

Don't be intimidated by the uniquely Persian elements of the recipes in this book. Getting to know new ingredients is fun and you can build up your Persian pantry over time as you try different dishes. Every ingredient you might need for Persian cooking is available in the U.S. these days, if not from your local supermarket, then from a Middle Eastern or Iranian store. Iranian markets are more common than you may think—most major cities have them; they tend to stock high-quality, fresh, seasonal ingredients, and are usually less expensive. Use the Internet to find the one nearest you or simply order what you need online. These specialty ingredients are also just a click away online, via websites such as Sadaf.com or Amazon. In this section, I've listed some of the items used in my recipes, including ones that you may not have in your pantry. ❧ In the recipes themselves, an asterisk by an ingredient or instruction for preparing something (such as grinding/infusing saffron), indicates that you can turn to this section for more details. ❧ I primarily use olive oil in my recipes—even for cooking rice and pastries—and fine-grain sea salt. Keep in mind that coarse grains will salt less because there are fewer of them in a given measure. On the other hand, ordinary table salt such as Morton iodized salt tends to salt more.

PERSIAN SPICE MIX

Ingredients for advieh, Persian spice mix, before grinding.

ADVIEH (PERSIAN SPICE MIX)

2 tablespoons dried rose petals
2 3-inch cinnamon sticks, crushed (to help grinding process)
2 tablespoons cardamom
2 tablespoons cumin
1 tablespoon ground golpar (Persian hogweed; whole seeds are hard to find)

In Persian, "advieh" refers both to spice in general and to a spice mix that Iranians either make themselves or buy ready-made. Families tend to create their own combinations. This one is mine; it makes just over ½ cup (30 g). Place all the spices together in a bowl, then transfer to a spice grinder or mortar and pestle, and grind to a powder. Store in an airtight glass container in a cool place to preserve freshness.

BARBERRIES (ZERESHK)

See pages 14–15.

BEANS, SOAKING, PEELING, + COOKING

Dried beans and legumes, such as fava, garbanzo (chickpea), and kidney, need to be soaked before cooking. The longer they are soaked, the less they need to be cooked. I prefer to soak my beans overnight. Place the dried beans in a large container, cover with water 2 in (5 cm) above the beans and allow to soak overnight. Rinse and drain.

SKINNING FRESH OR FROZEN FAVA BEANS: For fresh fava beans in the pod, split the pods open and remove the beans. Using a sharp paring knife, remove the little "hat" on top of each fava bean and squeeze the bean out of its skin. Alternatively, you can remove the skins by blanching the fava beans in the same way as for peeling tomatoes below. For frozen fava beans, soak in warm water for 5 minutes and then peel by simply squeezing the beans out of their skins.

CARDAMOM (HEL)

This widely available, tangy-tasting spice, a member of the ginger family, is native to India; traveling via caravan routes, it became a favorite in Iran, Greece, and Rome by classical times. Cardamom is sold whole in the form of dried green, white, or black pods. I use the green pods because they are unbleached. Within the pods are tiny, black, fragrant seeds. For recipes specifying ground cardamom, grind the whole pods: skin and seeds. There is no need to separate them.

BARBERRIES (*ZERESHK*)

Barberries are one of the specialties of Persian cooking. When choosing dried barberries, available from Iranian markets, be sure to select ones that are still red and not too dark, as these may be old. Dried barberries contain a lot of sand and so need to be washed properly: First remove the stems and pick over for grains of sand and grit. Place the barberries in a colander set in a large bowl of water and leave to soak for 15 minutes. Lift the colander out of the bowl, rinse thoroughly, and set aside.

TO CARAMELIZE BARBERRIES:

In a wide skillet, place 1 cup (150 grams) washed barberries, 1 tablespoon grape molasses or sugar, 2 tablespoons oil, and 2 tablespoons water, and stir-fry over medium heat for 4 minutes, until caramelized (taking care as barberries burn easily). You can store the caramelized berries in an airtight glass container in the fridge for 3 days or in the freezer for 3 weeks.

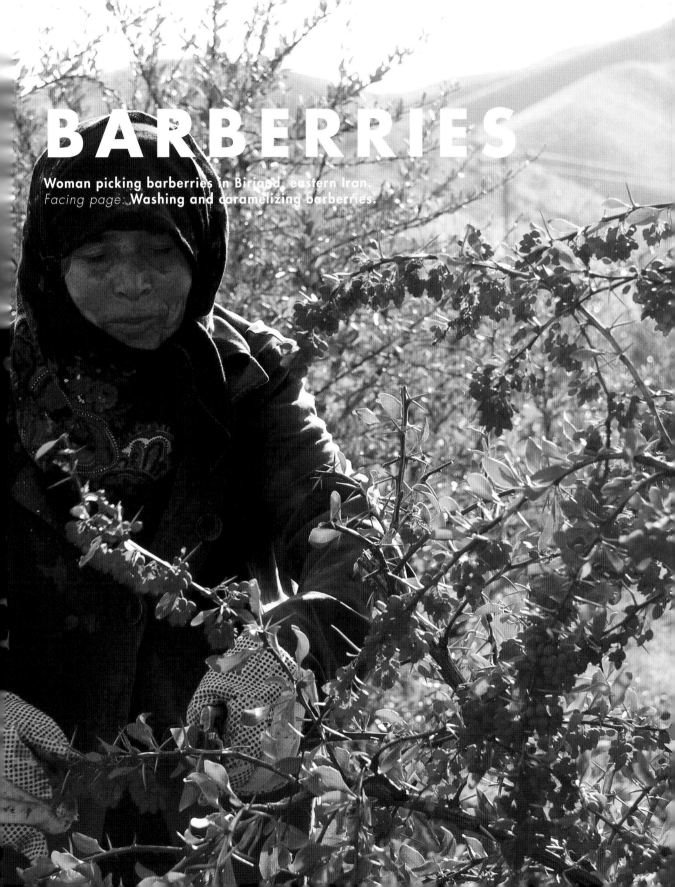

BARBERRIES

Woman picking barberries in Birjand, eastern Iran.
Facing page: Washing and caramelizing barberries.

CUCUMBERS, PERSIAN

Persian cucumbers are increasingly available in the U.S. Safeway, Whole Foods, and Trader Joe's have them. Our local farmers' market sells them fresh off the vine. Iranian markets also stock them throughout the year. They tend to be tastier and more delicate than the standard long cucumbers. Iranians eat them, peeled and with a little salt, as a fruit, as well as in salads.

EGGPLANTS, SALTING

Long, thin Japanese or Chinese eggplants are not bitter and so don't need to be salted. The larger Italian variety, a darker purple in color, can be quite bitter (I've found that the darker the eggplant the more bitter the skin) and will need to be salted to remove any bitterness. Peel the eggplants, slice, and soak in a large container of cold water with 2 tablespoons of salt for 20 minutes. Drain, rinse, and thoroughly blot dry.

PERSIAN HOGWEED (GOLPAR)

See pages 18–19.

GRAPE MOLASSES + VERJUICE

An excellent and tasty sweetener for any kitchen, grape molasses is essential in Persian cooking. Indeed, I often replace sugar with grape molasses. At the other end of the spectrum, made from unripe grapes, is the souring agent verjuice, essential in certain Persian dishes for its distinctive flavor.

HERBS

Buy your herbs and vegetables fresh as you need them. If you have the space in your garden, it's wonderful to grow herbs and basic vegetables if you can. I always grow my own Persian basil (also called anise basil, *O. basilicum* 'Licorice') from seed, available at Iranian markets. Plant them as early as possible depending on your geographic region and they will supply you well into October. There are, however, instances where the dried versions are more aromatic: dried mint and fenugreek leaves, for example.

(HERBS CONTINUED ON PAGE 20)

PERSIAN BASIL

Persian basil growing in a pot in the backyard.

PERSIAN
HOGWEED

PERSIAN HOGWEED (GOLPAR)

Golpar (*Heracleum persicum*), known as "Persian hogweed" in English, is a flowering plant native to Iran. Its seeds add a delightful aroma and zesty taste to many Persian dishes, especially those that contain pomegranates or fish. The powdered seeds are sold at Iranian markets (and via websites such as Amazon.com), but they are often mislabeled "angelica" or "marjoram," so it's best to ask for "golpar" to ensure you get the right ingredient. The photo on the right shows the dried seeds, which are kept whole when added to pickle preparations, but ground for use as a condiment. I love to use it, mixed with turmeric, as a spice rub for fish.

Left: Persian hogweed (golpar),ready for harvest on the foothills of the Alborz mountain range in northern Iran.
Right: The dried seeds before grinding.

(HERBS CONTINUED FROM PAGE 16)

WASHING HERBS for use in Persian cooking is very important. Great quantities are used and they need to be thoroughly cleaned, both to remove bacteria and to get rid of any unwelcome specks of sand or grit. They should also be dried completely before chopping. To wash the herbs, place them in a colander or salad-spinner basket set in a large container of water, add 2 tablespoons of vinegar, and allow to soak for 15 minutes. Lift up the basket and change the water several times until it is clear and no sand or sediment remains. Drain. Use the salad spinner to dry the herbs and place them on a sheet pan lined with paper towels. Allow them to *dry completely* at room temperature before chopping.

CHOPPING HERBS: In Persian cooking, for soups, kukus, braises, and rice dishes, the stems and stalks of cilantro, parsley, and spinach are chopped with the leaves. I use a chopping board and cleaver to finely chop my herbs, but you can also use a food processor. First cut a bunch of washed and thoroughly dried herbs into 3 parts, to make it easier for the food processor, and pulse. *Do not over-pulse*: you want them chopped, not juiced.

KASHK (DRIED BUTTERMILK)

In Iran, kashk is used in cooking as a high-protein, fat-free replacement for cream. Traditionally, kashk is sold dried and then reconstituted in water before use. These days it is also available fresh in liquid form and stored in the fridge. I recommend using it in this form, available from Iranian markets.

LIMES, DRIED PERSIAN

Dried Persian limes (*limu-omani*, or "limes from Oman") can be found in Iranian markets. They have a distinctive taste that is quite different from fresh lime. Dried lime powder (*gard-e limu-omani*), made from limes grown in California, is apt to be bitter because it contains ground seeds; I recommend using whole limes, but be sure to pierce them with the point of a knife in several places before adding them to the recipe.

MUSIR (PERSIAN SHALLOT)

See pages 22–23.

DRIED PERSIAN LIMES

PERSIAN
SHALLOTS

MUSIR (PERSIAN SHALLOT)

Also known as the Persian shallot, musir (*Allium hirtifolium* or *stipitatum*) is like a cross between elephant garlic and regular shallots. They grow wild in the foothills of the Zagros mountains. Musir has a deliciously unique taste, especially when mixed with yogurt. Dried musir is available in Iranian markets. It is best soaked overnight, then drained, rinsed with cold water, and patted dry before chopping finely.

Facing page: **Persian shallot field by lake Gohar in Lorestan.**
Right: **Harvesting the wild shallots.**

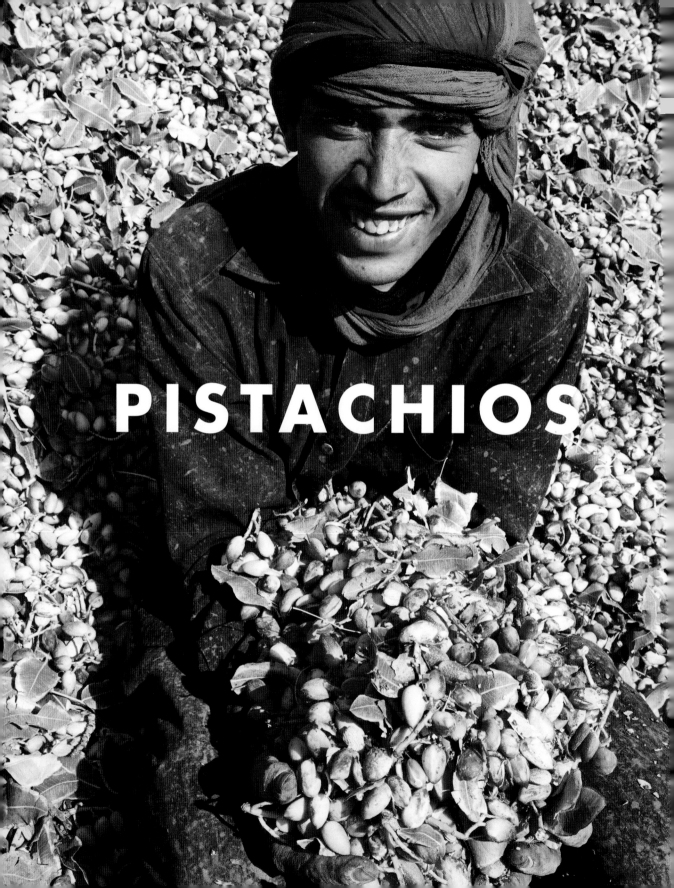

PISTACHIOS

PISTACHIOS

Persians were known as pistachio eaters as far back as the sixth century BCE. As a snack there is nothing better than a handful of roasted, salted, lemony pistachios in the shell. For cooking, I use raw California-grown pistachio kernels, which are now widely available in supermarkets in the U.S. Some of my recipes call for slivered pistachios, which can be harder to find. You can buy them at Iranian markets or via the Internet (at Sadaf.com), however, or make your own by cutting the raw kernels lengthways.

Facing page: A young Iranian farmer holding a cluster of fresh pistachios during the harvest in September in Rafsanjan, Iran.
Top right: Roasted and salted pistachios in the shell, raw pistachio kernels, and slivered pistachios.

RICE

NUTS + SEEDS, DRY-TOASTING

Heat a large skillet over medium heat, without any oil, and add the nuts/seeds. Cook, shaking the pan occasionally, for 5 to 10 minutes, or until golden brown. Store in an airtight jar. You can dry-toast walnuts in the oven: Spread them out in a rimmed sheet pan and place on the center rack of the oven (preheated to 350°F/180°C). Bake for 10 minutes, checking from time to time as they burn easily.

OILS

These days, I use olive oil in almost all my cooking, even for sautéing and for making pastries. I use less aromatic olive oils for cooking and a good virgin variety for salads and sauces.

PEPPER

For cooking, I use black peppercorns and grind them as needed. I also have a grinder set to grind coarsely and use it filled with a 4-color pepper blend for adding flavor and color to salads and dips.

PISTACHIOS

See spread on pages 24–25.

POMEGRANATES

See spread on pages 28–29.

PUMPKINS, CUTTING UP

Pumpkins and acorn and butternut squashes can all be prepared in the same way. With a heavy cleaver, slice the pumpkin or squash crosswise into 2 in (5 cm) rings. Remove the seeds with a spoon and discard. Use the cleaver to peel each section of pumpkin, then cut each section into 1 in (2.5 cm) cubes. Rinse and drain the cubes, and pat dry.

RICE

My favorite rice, a smoked variety from around the Caspian (*berenj-e dudi-e hashemi*), is hard to find, even in Iran. But Indian basmati rice, long-grained and wonderfully aromatic (its name comes from the Sanskrit *vasmati*, meaning "fragrant"), is excellent in Persian cooking.

(RICE CONTINUED ON PAGE 34)

To seed a pomegranate: Slice off the crown with a sharp knife. Make a superficial spiral cut in the skin around the pomegranate. Press both thumbs into the open crown and pull the fruit apart. Hold each segment over a bowl, with the seed side facing down, and tap the skin with a heavy spatula to dislodge the arils (seeds) from the membrane that holds them. The arils will fall through your fingers into the bowl.

POMEGRANATES

I love pomegranates—everything about them. And I try to use them in any way I can. Sometimes I even throw a pomegranate-themed party. I lay the table with a white cloth and Persian blue plates and make a centerpiece using pomegranate fruits and leaves from my garden. I start the meal by serving small bowls of pomegranate arils (seeds) sprinkled with a little salt and golpar. I then serve pomegranate soup (page 88) followed by a vegetarian version of the iconic fesenjan (pomegranate and walnut khoresh (page 178), accompanied by jeweled rice (page 183) and chicken kababs (page 143), and end with a delicious dessert of pomegranate granita (page 207) served over frozen yogurt. These days pomegranate arils are used more and more; indeed, I'm often asked how to seed pomegranates, see the facing page for an easy way to do this. For pomegranate juice, it's best to make your own using the fresh fruit. If using bottled pomegranate juice, be sure to buy the pure kind, and not from concentrate. In my recipes, I also use pomegranate molasses and paste—the Sadaf brand of pomegranate molasses has a perfect balance of sweet and sour.

THE PERSIAN ROSE

Picking rose petals in Qamsar, Iran

The name for "flower" and "rose" is the same in Persian—*gol*. Ancient Iranians valued roses not only for their beauty and perfume, but also for their use in medicine and cooking. It was in the fourth century BCE that Alexander the Great introduced the rose from Iran to Greece, sending specimens to Aristotle for cultivating in his botanical gardens in Athens. From there, the rose spread further West. Rose petals and rose water have been part of Persian cooking since ancient times, used in savory as well as sweet dishes. These days, they are used mostly in sweet pastries, though in some villages in Iran they are still incorporated in savory dishes. I love to use them in all of my cooking. I keep a bag of rose petals and a bottle of rose water handy in the kitchen for use in a range of recipes. I add rose water to my rice and braises, as well as to pastries, and I use dried rose petals to add taste and texture to salads and desserts. They are also one of the ingredients in my Persian spice mix (advieh, page 13). Buy the dried petals (don't use buds) and crush them in your hand as you sprinkle them in a recipe.

SAFFRON

Saffron is made from the dried orange stigmas of the saffron crocus. When buying the spice, choose threads rather than powder (which is too often adulterated with turmeric). Saffron threads need to be ground before using. Iranian saffron (sold in small quantities of 1 mesqal/4.7g) is the best. Here's how to prepare saffron for cooking. Using a mortar and pestle or a spice grinder, grind the threads into a powder with 1 sugar cube (the sugar absorbs the moisture and helps the grinding process). Use 1 teaspoon of the ground saffron (if you have more, store it in an airtight glass container in the freezer). Then, in a glass container, dissolve 1 teaspoon of saffron powder in ¼ cup (60 ml) hot water. For even more flavor, you can use rose water or orange blossom water instead of hot water. Store in an airtight glass bottle in the fridge for up to 3 weeks and use as needed.

SAFFRON

Saffron crocuses in the field in Qaenat in eastern Iran.

It is widely available in the U.S., even in supermarkets. Iranian and other Middle Eastern grocers have several brands of basmati rice.

If you are using aged Indian basmati rice, it is best to wash it first as this greatly improves its wonderful aroma. Place the rice in a large container and cover with water. Allow to soak for 30 minutes. Drain in a fine-meshed colander, then rinse thoroughly before using. Long-grain rice grown in America doesn't need to be washed.

ROSE WATER / PETALS

See pages 30–31.

SAFFRON

See pages 32–33.

SALT

I use two types of salt: fine-grained sea salt for most cooking, and flakes of salt (or fleur de sel, as the French call it—Maldon is a good brand) for sprinkling over kababs and eggs. Bear in mind that the coarser the grain the less it salts, especially if you use a coarse-grained variety such as kosher salt. Avoid the regular Morton salt as it's a bit too strong. If that's all you have, use less for the recipes in this book; it's best to taste as you go, and experiment.

SPRING ONIONS (SCALLIONS)

I use spring onions in many recipes—all of it, both the white and green parts; it's a favorite ingredient in Iranian cooking. I prefer "spring onion" to "scallion," although it is exactly the same thing, because it sounds fresher—just like the onion itself.

SUMAC (*SOMAQ, RUHS CORIARIA*)

Sumac has a distinctive lemony taste. The berry clusters are harvested in September, hung to dry then ground. The powdered form is used as a condiment, mostly on kababs, but also in soups and on meatballs. I've also used it with fish, including a delicious recipe for sumac-coated fish (page 130).

SUMAC

Sumac berries ready for harvest

TOMATOES, PEELING

There is little to equal the taste of fresh, ripe tomatoes in season; out of season, peeled, canned tomatoes make a good substitute. In my kitchen, I always peel tomatoes. If you are using more than one, it is simpler to remove the skin by blanching (parboiling and then refreshing in iced water) than with a knife or peeler. First bring a pot of water to a boil. Place a large bowl of iced water next to you. Next make a shallow circular cut to remove the greenish-white crown on top of each tomato. Gently drop the tomatoes into the boiling water and leave for no longer than 20 to 30 seconds, just until the skin begins to peel away. Use a slotted spoon or spider to remove the tomatoes and lower them into the iced water. Lift them from the water, place on a sheet pan or plate, and peel off the skins, which will come away easily.

TURMERIC (*ZARDCHUBEH*)

Turmeric comes from the rhizomes of a plant in the ginger family, a native of southeast Asia that is now grown throughout the world in countries with a tropical climate. Although fresh turmeric is sometimes available (our farmers' market has it in October), it is hard to find. Ready-ground turmeric makes a perfectly good alternative, however.

VINEGARS

I keep 5 different types of vinegar in my kitchen: a red wine vinegar (sherry vinegar); rice vinegar; balsamic vinegar, including a white balsamic vinegar (it adds a great taste to salad dressings without darkening them); and an apple cider vinegar (I add splashes of it to the water for washing fresh herbs and salads, especially from the garden or farmers' market).

YOGURT, DRAINING + THICKENING

Yogurt is traditionally thickened by placing it in a muslin bag, or 3 layers of cheesecloth, then hanging it up and leaving it to drain overnight. A shortcut is to put the yogurt in a bowl on a rimmed sheet pan, and place 3 or 4 layers of paper towel on top with the sides hanging down. The paper towels absorb the excess liquid, which then drains onto the pan under the bowl. Leave to drain for 1 to 2 hours, after which the yogurt will have thickened. Cover and store the drained yogurt in the fridge. Thick yogurt is available in supermarkets under the name "labneh." Labneh, which is often mislabeled as cheese, is also available in Persian markets, where they have the Iranian variety as well, called "*mast-e chekideh* or *mast-e khiky.*"

TURMERIC

Ground turmeric with fresh root—whole and grated

PREPARING TO COOK
mise en place

Setting out your prepared ingredients, known as *mise en place* in French, is standard practice in professional kitchens, but I would recommend it for anyone who wants to cook with less hassle. Before I cook, I put all the ingredients I'll need for a recipe, measured out and placed in small bowls or other containers, on a large, rimmed sheet pan. For example, the photo on the facing page is the *mise en place* for Fresh Herb Kuku (page 104). This has two advantages: first, you will know well in advance if you are missing any ingredients; secondly, it speeds up the cooking process. Nonetheless, keep in mind that when a dish is ready to serve, you should adjust the seasoning to your taste. ☙ For the recipes in this book I have given measurements primarily in the form of cup or spoon measures, but with weights (metric) in brackets. In some places—such as for uncut meat and vegetables—I have provided weights only.

SMALL DISHES TO MIX + MATCH

In this section you'll find a number of refreshing yogurt-based dishes as well as spreads and various vegan and vegetarian salads made from a whole range of different ingredients, from lentils, bulgur and chickpeas to kale, beets and even persimmons. The traditional Iranian way of serving a meal is to have one main dish (or more) accompanied by many small dishes on the table. Everyone then helps themselves according to their fancy. There is no particular order regarding what you might eat or when. Together with these dishes there is usually a green platter consisting of Persian basil, cheese, radishes, spring onions, and walnuts. This is accompanied by hot, crispy, flat Persian bread. Iranians often begin (and end) a meal by using a piece of the flat bread to make a mouthful from this platter. ❧ Later sections in this book cover egg-based kukus, meatballs, and turnovers, which can also be placed on the table as small side dishes.

Serves 4
Prep: 15 minutes

3 Persian cucumbers,* or
   1 long seedless cucumber,
   peeled and grated
3 cups (735 g) plain, thick
   yogurt or labneh*
2 spring onions (white and
   green parts), chopped
2 tablespoons chopped fresh
   mint, or 1 teaspoon dried
   mint
2 tablespoons chopped fresh
   dill weed
2 tablespoons chopped fresh
   tarragon, or 1 teaspoon
   dried tarragon
1 clove garlic, peeled and
   grated
1 teaspoon sea salt
1 teaspoon freshly ground
   pepper
3 tablespoons chopped
   walnuts (optional)

GARNISH
½ cup (75 g) seedless raisins
Sprigs of fresh mint
Sprigs of fresh dill weed
1 tablespoon dried rose
   petals*
1 radish, diced

What I love about this salad is that it's so easy to make, so classically Persian in taste, and yet so modern. What's more, it's a complete meal for vegetarians. I prefer to use thick Persian yogurt or labneh.

1. Combine all the salad ingredients in a mixing bowl. Mix thoroughly, adjust the seasoning to taste, and garnish.

2. Mix in the garnish and serve with toasted bread or as a side dish. *Nush-e joon!*

NOTE

In the summer, this yogurt salad can be transformed into a wonderfully refreshing cold soup by adding 1 cup cold water and 2 or 3 ice cubes. Add more salt and pepper to taste. You can also crumble toasted bread or croutons into the soup just before serving. My husband increases the amount of raisins and adds more ice and water to make a very thin but delicious version of this cold soup.

YOGURT + CUCUMBER SALAD

mast-o khiar

YOGURT + SPINACH BORANI

borani-e esfenaj

Serves 4
Prep: 10 minutes
Cooking: 30 minutes

YOGURT + SPINACH SALAD

Iranians are very fond of vegetables mixed with yogurt. They are called "borani." Here, I am giving you a spinach borani, but you can use other greens such as purslane, kale, or even lettuce.

2 tablespoons olive oil

2 large onions, peeled and thinly sliced

4 cloves garlic, peeled and chopped

1 lb (450 g) fresh spinach, washed and chopped, or 1½ cups (350 g) frozen spinach, thawed and chopped

¼ cup (20 g) chopped fresh cilantro

¼ cup (20 g) chopped fresh mint

1½ cups (365 g) plain, thick yogurt or labneh*

½ teaspoon sea salt

¼ teaspoon freshly ground pepper

GARNISH (OPTIONAL)

1/8 teaspoon ground saffron dissolved in 1 tablespoon hot water*

1. In a wide skillet, heat the oil over medium heat. Add the onions and garlic, and sauté for 20 minutes, stirring occasionally to prevent burning, until the onions are soft and browned.

2. Add the spinach, cilantro, and mint, cover, and steam for 3 to 5 minutes, or until the spinach is wilted.

3. Remove from heat and allow to cool for 10 to 15 minutes before transferring to a serving bowl.

4. Add the yogurt, salt, and pepper, and mix well. Add the garnish according to your fancy.

5. Serve with other vegetables or lavash bread. *Nush-e joon!*

VE
VEGETARIAN

Serves 4
Prep: 30 minutes
Cooking: 15 minutes

FAVA BEAN SALAD

3lb (1.3kg) fresh fava beans in the pod or 1lb (450g) frozen fava beans, second skin removed*

4 tablespoons olive oil

2 cloves garlic, peeled and grated

1½ teaspoons sea salt

¼ teaspoon freshly ground pepper

1 tablespoon fresh lime juice

½ cup (45 g) chopped fresh dill weed

1 teaspoon ground golpar* (optional)

½ cup (120 g) plain yogurt (optional)

Fava beans (also called broad beans) travelled along the Silk Road from Iran to China. Traditionally, Iranians eat fresh fava beans cooked in the pod with a little salt and sprinkled with golpar, much like the way the Japanese eat edamame. However, I recently tasted this recipe in Tabriz in northwest Iran, where they used fresh, young, green fava beans, dill and garlic. It makes a perfect dish for vegans. For everyone else, thick plain yogurt or goat cheese mixed in is also delicious.

1. Shell the fresh fava beans from their pods.

2. To remove the second skins: In a medium saucepan, bring 8 cups water and 1 teaspoon salt to a boil. Add the shelled fava beans and blanch for 30 seconds. Drain immediately and allow to cool. When cool enough to handle, use your fingers to remove the hat on top of the beans and then push them out of their second skins. Set them aside.

3. Heat the oil in a wide skillet over medium heat. Add the garlic, fava beans, salt and pepper, and sauté for 1 minute. Add the lime juice, golpar, and dill, and give it a stir.

4. Adjust the seasoning to taste, and transfer to a serving bowl. Garnish with yogurt, if you wish, and stir gently. This salad is excellent with eggs, rice or quinoa. *Nush-e joon!*

NOTE

If you use frozen fava beans with second skins already removed (available at Iranian markets), remove from the package, place in a colander, rinse with warm water, and drain completely. Then begin the recipe with step 3 above.

NOTE ON THE PHOTO

I have garnished the dish with some wonderfully delicate cilantro flowers from my backyard.

FAVA BEAN SALAD

borani-e baqala sabz

YOGURT + PERSIAN SHALLOT DIP

mast-o musir

Serves 6
Prep: 15 minutes, plus soaking
 for 3 hours

YOGURT + PERSIAN SHALLOT DIP

1½ cups (135 g) dried musir
 (Persian shallots)*
4 cups (960 g) strained, plain
 whole yogurt or *labneh* (a
 creamy strained yogurt)
1 teaspoon sea salt
½ teaspoon freshly ground
 pepper
1 cup (85 g) shredded fresh
 mint, or 1 tablespoon dried
 mint

GARNISH (OPTIONAL)
1 teaspoon crushed dried
 rose petals*
1 tablespoon fresh mint
 leaves

Dried Persian shallots (musir) are available in Iranian markets, and well worth the effort it might take to buy them. I think of them like truffles – they grow wild in the foothills of the Zagros Mountains, and have to be found and dug out of the earth by dedicated artisans (see page 23). This lovely, simple dish is great to have in your fridge at all times (it will keep, covered, in the fridge, for a week). It goes to perfection with eggs and every kind of kabab, adding a wonderful and distinctive flavor to any dish it accompanies.

1. Soak the musir in water for 3 to 24 hours in the fridge. Drain, rinse in cold water, and pat dry. Inspect the soaked musir, cutting out any stems that remain hard after soaking, and chop finely.

2. In a mixing bowl, combine the chopped musir with the yogurt, salt, pepper, and mint. Mix well.

3. Add the garnish if you like and serve as an appetizer or an accompaniment. *Nush-e joon!*

VE
VEGETARIAN

Serves 4
Prep: 15 minutes
Cooking: 1 hour

EGGPLANT, MINT + WALNUT SPREAD

2–3 large eggplants
(about 2½ lb/1.1 kg)
4 tablespoons olive oil
2 large onions, peeled and
thinly sliced
6 cloves garlic, sliced
1½ teaspoon sea salt
½ teaspoon freshly ground
pepper
1 teaspoon turmeric
1 cup (85 g) ground walnuts
1 tablespoon dried mint
2/3 cup (160 g) liquid kashk*

GARNISH (OPTIONAL)
⅛ teaspoon ground saffron
dissolved in 1 tablespoon
hot water*
1 tablespoon plain liquid
kashk*
Fresh mint leaves

You can make this recipe 24 hours in advance and store it, covered, in the fridge. Reheat or allow it to get to room temperature before serving. If you replace the kashk with tahini paste (raw sesame paste), you'll have a perfect vegan dish.

1. Roast the eggplants on all sides over a cooktop flame until the skin is burnt and completely blackened. If you don't have a gas cooktop, preheat the oven to 450°F (230°C). Halve the eggplants lengthwise. Place them, skin side down, on an oiled rack in a rimmed sheet pan, and bake in the oven for 1 hour.

2. Place the eggplants on a chopping board and leave them until cool enough to handle. Remove and discard the skins, and finely chop the eggplant.

3. Heat the oil in a wide, deep skillet over medium heat. Add the onions and garlic and sauté for 15 minutes, stirring occasionally, until golden brown. Add the salt, pepper, turmeric, chopped eggplants, ground walnuts, and ½ cup water, and stir well. Cover and cook over medium heat for 5 to 10 minutes, until all the juices have been absorbed and the eggplant is tender.

4. Mix-in the mint and kashk. Adjust seasoning to taste and transfer to a serving dish. Garnish and serve warm—or at room temperature—with bread, fresh basil and mint. Or serve as a side dish. *Nush-e joon!*

EGGPLANT + POMEGRANATE SPREAD

1. In step 3, add 1 peeled and diced medium tomato.

2. In step 4, replace the kashk with 1 tablespoon pomegranate molasses, 1 teaspoon grape molasses, and 1 teaspoon golpar.

3. Garnish with leaves of basil, mint, or cilantro, and pomegranate arils.

EGGPLANT + MINT & WALNUT SPREAD

borani-e bademjan

Serves 4
Prep: 15 minutes
Cooking: 50 minutes

1 teaspoon sea salt
½ teaspoon freshly ground
   pepper
1 teaspoon turmeric
1 tablespoon cumin seeds
1 large head of cauliflower,
   rinsed and broken into
   florets
4 tablespoons olive oil

OPTIONAL
4 slices Emmental, or your
   favorite semi-hard, cheese

ROASTED CAULIFLOWER + CUMIN

I love this simple dish full of taste and flavor. It makes a perfect appetizer or side dish.

1. line a rimmed baking sheet with parchment paper. Preheat oven to 450°F (230°C). In a small bowl, place the salt, pepper, turmeric, and cumin seeds, and mix well.

2. Place the cauliflowers on the sheet pan. Drizzle with the olive oil, and sprinkle with the salt mixture. Toss well and spread evenly.

3. Roast in the oven for 45 to 50 minutes, until golden brown.

4. If you wish, pull out the rack and arrange the cheese slices on top of the cauliflower florets. Return it to the oven and bake for another 5 minutes until the cheese has melted completely.

5. Remove from the oven and allow to cool for few minutes in order to handle the parchment paper. Transfer the cauliflowers with the parchment paper to a serving dish *Nush-e joon!*

Serves 4
Prep: 15 minutes
Cooking: 25 minutes

1 pound (450 g) cubanelle,
   shishito or mini peppers
5 cloves garlic smashed
2 tablespoons olive oil
½ teaspoon sea salt
½ teaspoon freshly ground
   pepper

ROASTED SWEET PEPPERS + GARLIC

This is a great and easy dish to make. You can use any of the varieties of sweet peppers. My favorites are cubanelle and shishito peppers.

1. line a rimmed baking sheet with parchment paper. Preheat oven to 450°F (230°C)

2. If using cubanelle peppers, cut them lengthwise into quarters. Spread the peppers, and garlic cloves on the sheet pan. Drizzle the olive oil and sprinkle the salt on top. Toss well. Roast in the oven for 15 to 25 minutes, until well roasted.

3. Remove from the oven and allow to cool for a few minutes so you can handle the parchment paper. Transfer the peppers with the parchment paper to a serving dish. *Nush-e joon!*

ROASTED CAULIFLOWER + CUMIN

gol-e kalam-e tanuri

Serves 4 to 6
Prep: 5 minutes, plus soaking
  the chickpeas overnight
Cooking: 30 minutes

CHICKPEA, SESAME + KALE SPREAD /GREEN HUMMUS

1 cup (200 g) dried chickpeas,
  soaked overnight* (also
  see note below)

4 kale leaves, thoroughly
  rinsed, center stems
  removed

2 cloves garlic, peeled and
  crushed

1½ teaspoons sea salt

1 teaspoon ground cumin

1 teaspoon cayenne

2 tablespoons tahini paste

1 tablespoon olive oil

5 tablespoons fresh lime
  juice

1 teaspoon grape molasses*
  or honey

½ cup (40 g) fresh parsley
  leaves

GARNISH

1 tablespoon olive oil

¼ teaspoon cayenne

½ cup (40 g) pomegranate
  arils (optional)

NOTE

You can replace the
dried chickpeas with
2 cups (400 g) canned,
cooked chickpeas, drained
and rinsed. Eliminate
step 1 and add the cooked
chickpeas and the raw kale
in step 2.

Hummus, which means "chickpea" in Arabic, first appeared in the royal kitchens of the Abbasid court (run by Persian chefs) in Baghdad in the ninth century. Since then it has spread throughout the Middle East and crossed international borders to become one of the most popular snacks around the world. Rightly so, as it's delicious, healthy, and very easy to make. Here, I have added kale and parsley, making it green, and even more tasty.

1. Place the soaked and drained chickpeas in a saucepan and add enough water to cover the chickpeas by 2½ in (6 cm). Bring to a boil, then reduce heat to medium, cover, and cook for 30 minutes, or until tender. Add the kale and bring back to a boil. Remove from heat and drain, saving ¼ cup (60 ml) of the cooking liquid.

2. Place the cooked chickpeas and kale mixture in the bowl of a food processor with the garlic, salt, cumin, cayenne, tahini, olive oil, lime juice, grape molasses, parsley, and the saved chickpea liquid. Mix until you have a thick, smooth purée.

3. Adjust the seasoning to taste, by adding extra lime juice or cayenne, transfer to a serving dish, and garnish. *Nush-e joon!*

NOTE

You can also make this spread with other kinds of bean, such as cannellini.

GREEN HUMMUS

halim-e nokhod

BUTTERNUT SQUASH + KASHK SPREAD

kashk-o kadu

Serves 6
Prep: 10 minutes
Cooking: 1 hour

BUTTERNUT SQUASH + KASHK SPREAD

1 large butternut squash
   (about 3 lb/1.3 kg)
2 tablespoons olive oil
2 large onions, peeled and
   thinly sliced
6 cloves garlic, peeled and
   sliced
1½ teaspoon sea salt
½ teaspoon freshly ground
   pepper
1 teaspoon turmeric
1 tablespoon dried mint
1 cup (85 g) ground walnuts
¾ cup (180 ml) liquid kashk*

GARNISH
1 cup fresh mint leaves
1 cup fresh basil leaves
2 tablespoons liquid kashk*

This recipe may be made up to 24 hours in advance and stored, covered, in the fridge. Reheat or allow it to get to room temperature before serving.

1. Preheat the oven to 450°F (230°C). Cut the butternut squash in half lengthwise and remove the seeds using a spoon.

2. Place an oiled rack in a rimmed pan sheet. Arrange the butternut squash halves, face side down, on the rack. Bake in the oven for 1 hour.

3. Remove the squash from the oven and leave until cool enough to handle.

4. Meanwhile, heat the oil in a large, deep skillet over medium heat. Add the onions and garlic and sauté for 15 minutes, or until golden brown. Add the salt, pepper, turmeric, and dried mint and stir-fry for 20 seconds.

5. Use a spoon to remove the flesh of the butternut squash, and add it to the onion mixture in the skillet. Add the ground walnuts and the kashk, mashing and mixing together until you have a smooth texture. Adjust the seasoning to taste.

6. Transfer the spread to a serving dish and garnish. Serve with bread or a tortilla (as a taco), and more fresh basil and mint, or as a side dish. *Nush-e joon!*

BEET, WALNUT + KASHK SPREAD

Replace the butternut squash with 3 pounds (1.3 kg) beets, everything else remains the same (if the beets are small, reduce cooking time to 45 minutes).

Serves 6
Prep: 30 minutes

8 oz (225 g) white goat-milk cheese (feta-type), rinsed, drained, and cut into small cubes

2 cups (240 g) shelled walnuts, toasted (see note)

2 spring onions (white and green parts), chopped

1 cup (85 g) fresh basil leaves

½ cup (40 g) fresh tarragon leaves

2 cups (170 g) fresh mint leaves

1 clove garlic, peeled

1 teaspoon sea salt

¼ teaspoon freshly ground pepper

Juice of 2 limes

½ cup (120 ml) olive oil

6in (15 cm) pita or any kind of flat bread, toasted and cut up

GARNISH

12 Persian cucumbers,* peeled and sliced lengthwise

6 large radishes, sliced

Traditionally Iranians have a platter of fresh green herbs, nuts, cheese and bread on the table throughout the meal. I highly recommend you try it at your next dinner. Here, however, I am reviving an old tradition, which feels deliciously modern. All the ingredients are thrown into a food processor and pulsed into a grainy paste. As bread is already included in the recipe, I would recommend eating it spread over slices of Persian cucumber and radishes. It is best made just before serving.

1. When you are ready to serve, place all the ingredients except the garnish in a food processor and pulse into a grainy paste.

2. Transfer the mixture to a serving bowl, place in the middle of a large platter and arrange the cucumber and radish slices around the bowl. *Nush-e joon!*

NOTE

To toast the walnuts: Preheat the oven to 350°F (180°C), place the walnuts on a rimmed sheet pan, and bake for 5 to 10 minutes, checking from time to time as they burn easily.

VE
VEGETARIAN

CHEESE, WALNUT + HERB SPREAD

doymaj

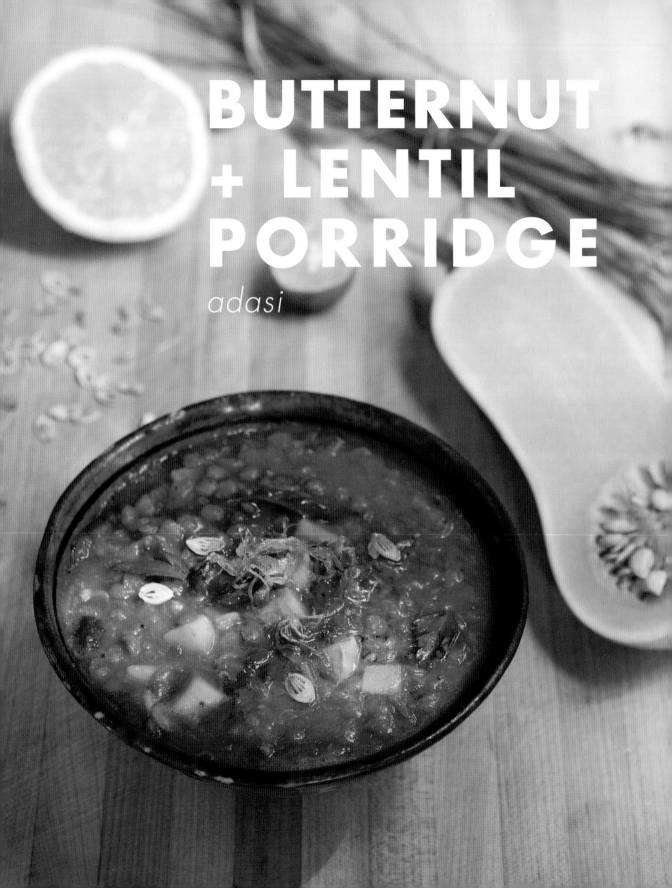

BUTTERNUT + LENTIL PORRIDGE

adasi

Serves 6 to 8
Prep: 20 minutes plus soaking
  the lentils overnight
Cooking: 1 hour

BUTTERNUT + LENTIL PORRIDGE

2 cups (400 g) brown lentils,
  soaked overnight, rinsed
  and drained*
2 tablespoons olive oil
1 tablespoon cumin seeds
2 large onions, peeled and
  thinly sliced
4 cloves garlic, peeled
8 oz (225 g) peeled butternut
  squash or pumpkin, cut
  into 1 in (2.5 cm) cubes*
1 tablespoon sea salt
½ teaspoon freshly ground
  pepper
½ teaspoon turmeric
8 cups (2.25 l) water
¼ teaspoon cayenne
½ teaspoon smoked paprika
1 tablespoon ground golpar*
2/3 cup (160 ml) Seville
  orange juice, or ½ cup
  (120 ml) fresh orange juice
  mixed with ½ cup (120 ml)
  fresh lime juice

GARNISH
1 cup (85 g) chopped fresh
  parsley

This is a delicious, easy to make, and very nutritious dish called adasi in Persian. Many restaurants have it on their menus in Iran these days. It may be made up to 24 hours in advance and stored in the fridge. Reheat before serving. Don't be put off by having to soak the lentils overnight—it's easy to do. All beans benefit from soaking, which considerably reduces their cooking time.

1. Heat the oil in a medium-sized, heavy pot over medium heat. Add the cumin seeds and stir-fry for 20 seconds, or until aromatic (keep a lid handy to cover the pan, if necessary, to stop any seeds from flying out).

2. Tip in the onions, garlic, and butternut squash and stir-fry for 10 minutes. Add the salt, pepper, turmeric, and lentils, and stir-fry for 20 seconds.

3. Pour in the water and bring to a boil. Reduce heat to medium, partially cover, and simmer, stirring occasionally, for about 40 minutes, or until the lentils are tender.

4. Use a handheld mixer to partially purée the lentils.

5. Add the cayenne, paprika, golpar, and Seville orange juice and bring back to a boil. Reduce heat to medium, cover partially, and simmer for another 10 minutes, stirring occasionally.

6. Adjust the seasoning to taste, cover, and keep warm until ready to serve. Just before serving, transfer to a bowl and garnish with the chopped parsley. *Nush-e joon!*

Serves 4
Prep: 10 minutes
Cooking: 30 to 45 minutes

LENTIL SALAD

1 cup (200 g) brown (or
   French) lentils, rinsed
6 cups (1.5 liters) water

DRESSING
1 cup (100 g) chopped spring
   onions (white and green
   parts)
1 clove garlic, peeled and
   grated
¼ cup rice vinegar or fresh
   lime juice
1 teaspoon sea salt
½ teaspoon freshly ground
   pepper
1 tablespoon ground cumin
½ cup (60 ml) olive oil

SALAD
2 tablespoons chopped fresh
   cilantro
½ bell pepper, seeded and
   diced small
½ red onion, peeled and
   diced small

Rich in protein, lentils have been popular in Iran since ancient times. I often make this salad for my son who is a vegan. You can make it with any kind of dried bean.

1. Place the lentils in a medium-heavy saucepan. Pour in the water and cook, uncovered, over medium heat for 30 to 45 minutes (depending on the type of lentils used), or until tender. Drain and set aside.

2. Meanwhile, in a salad bowl, whisk together all the ingredients for the dressing.

3. Add the cooked, drained and still warm lentils, and all the salad ingredients and toss together thoroughly.

4. Adjust the seasoning, adding more salt, vinegar or olive oil to taste. Serve over a bed of green-leaf lettuce, with toasted flat bread, or as a side dish. *Nush-e joon!*

LENTIL SALAD
salad-e adasi

CUCUMBER + POMEGRANATE SALAD

salad-e khiar-o anar

Serves 4
Prep: 25 minutes

CUCUMBER + POMEGRANATE SALAD

DRESSING
Juice of 1 lime
¼ cup (60 ml) olive oil
1 teaspoon sea salt
½ teaspoon freshly ground
pepper
1 teaspoon ground golpar*
(optional)

SALAD
½ cup (75 g) peeled and
diced red onions
½ cup (40 g) chopped fresh
mint, or 1 tablespoon dried
mint
6 Persian cucumbers,* or
2 long seedless cucumbers,
peeled and diced
Arils of 2 pomegranates
(about 1 cup/150 g)

This traditional Persian tribal salad is usually made with just dried mint and vinegar. Here, I have somewhat elaborated on the original recipe. Served with cheese, walnuts, and toasted bread, it makes an excellent meal.

1. In a serving bowl, whisk together all the ingredients for the dressing.

2. Just before serving, add all the ingredients for the salad and toss lightly. Season to taste with extra salt and lime juice. *Nush-e joon!*

TOMATO, CUCUMBER + MINT SALAD

DRESSING

1 tablespoon olive oil
1 tablespoon fresh lime juice
2 tablespoons rice vinegar
1 clove garlic, peeled and
  grated
½ teaspoon fine sea salt
¼ teaspoon freshly ground
  pepper

SALAD

2 firm ripe tomatoes, peeled
  and diced*
6 Persian cucumbers,* or
  2 long seedless cucumbers,
  peeled and diced
2 spring onions (white and
  green parts), chopped
3 radishes, sliced
2 tablespoons chopped fresh
  parsley
2 tablespoons chopped fresh
  mint
2 tablespoons chopped fresh
  cilantro

For this renowned salad from Shiraz, the ingredients are traditionally diced very finely and only lime juice—no olive oil—is used in the dressing. It is eaten with everything, much like a salsa. I prefer to dice the ingredients a little larger and add olive oil as well as rice vinegar to the dressing. You can prepare the ingredients and the dressing a little in advance but do not add the dressing until you are ready to serve this salad. For a variation on this salad, popular in the Middle East, add 1 tablespoon sumac; a small bell pepper, seeded and diced; and 1 cup crispy croutons.

1. Just before serving, in a salad bowl, whisk together all the ingredients for the dressing.

2. Add the diced tomatoes and cucumber with the remaining vegetables and herbs, and toss well. Serve immediately. *Nush-e joon!*

TOMATO + CUCUMBER + MINT SALAD

Shirazi Salad

CHICKPEA, CILANTRO + CUMIN SALAD

Salad-e Nokhod

Serves 4
Prep: 15 minutes, plus soaking
  the chickpeas overnight
Cooking: 55 minutes

CHICKPEA, CILANTRO + CUMIN SALAD

1 cup (200 g) dried chickpeas, soaked in water overnight, and drained
8 cups (1.9 liters) water
¼ cup (60 ml) olive oil
1 tablespoon cumin seeds
1 small red onion, peeled and finely chopped
1 clove garlic, peeled and chopped
1 in (2½ cm) fresh ginger root, peeled and grated
½ teaspoon sea salt
½ teaspoon freshly ground pepper
1 hot green chili (such as jalapeño), chopped, or ⅛ teaspoon cayenne
1 tablespoon fresh lime juice
1 tablespoon tomato paste
1 large tomato, peeled* and diced
½ cup (40 g) chopped fresh cilantro

BED OF GREENS
4 cups (340 g) shredded greens (such as romaine lettuce or arugula)

1. Place the chickpeas in a medium-sized saucepan. Add 8 cups of water and bring to a boil. Reduce heat to medium, partially cover, and cook for 30 to 40 minutes, or until the chickpeas are tender. Drain and set aside.

2. Meanwhile, heat the oil in a wide, deep skillet over a medium heat until very hot. Add the cumin, tip in the onion and garlic, and stir-fry for 5 to 10 minutes, or until the onions are lightly golden.

3. Add the cooked chickpeas and all the remaining ingredients except for the cilantro and stir-fry for 5 minutes.

4. Stir in the cilantro and adjust seasoning to taste.

5. You can serve this on a bed of greens with bread, rice, pasta, or bulgur, according to your fancy.

_____
VARIATION

You can replace the chickpeas with the same quantity of dried black beans, kidney beans, or white beans, or a mixture of all three.

Serves 4
Prep: 30 minutes, plus soaking
   for 1 hour

BULGUR SALAD / TABBOULEH

This is a wonderful, classic Middle Eastern salad. In Turkey, where it is called kisir, it is made with half the quantity of parsley and a dressing sharpened by pomegranate molasses (¼ cup/60 ml in this instance) instead of the lime juice.

SALAD

1 cup (180 g) fine-grained bulgur (cracked wheat), rinsed in a fine-mesh colander

¼ cup (60 ml) boiling water

3 cups (255 g) finely chopped flat-leaf parsley

½ cup (40 g) chopped fresh mint

½ jalapeño pepper, seeded and diced (optional)

4 Persian cucumbers,* or 1 long seedless cucumber, cut into ½ in (1 cm) cubes

4 spring onions (white and green parts), finely chopped

4 medium tomatoes, peeled* and diced into ¼ in (5 mm) cubes

DRESSING

1 clove garlic, peeled and grated

2/3 cup (160 ml) fresh lime juice

2/3 cup (160 ml) olive oil

½ teaspoon honey

1½ teaspoons sea salt

1 teaspoon freshly ground pepper

BED OF GREENS

4 little gem or romaine lettuce hearts, or endives

1. Place the bulgur in a large salad bowl and stir in the ¼ cup boiling water. Cover tightly with plastic wrap and allow to soak for 1 hour. The bulgur should be tender.

2. Meanwhile, prepare the rest of the salad ingredients.

3. In a small bowl, whisk together all the ingredients for the dressing.

4. Add the salad ingredients to the soaked bulgur in the salad bowl.

5. Pour the salad dressing over the salad. Toss well and adjusting the seasoning to taste.

6. Create a bed of lettuce leaves on each individual plate and place the bulgur salad in the center. Another good way to serve this dish is to use the romaine lettuce leaves for scooping up the salad.

NOTE

You can soak the bulgur the night before, cover and keep in the fridge overnight.

TABBOULEH

salad-e balghur

CURLY KALE + PERSIMMON SALAD

salad-e kayl-o khormalu

Serves 4
Prep: 30 minutes

CURLY KALE + PERSIMMON SALAD

SALAD

2 lb (900 g) curly kale, center stalks removed. As the kale leaves can have bits of sand and other particles attached, it is important to wash and dry them thoroughly before shredding.

4 Chinese persimmons (round and firm)

1 cup (140 g) pumpkin seeds

DRESSING

1 cloves garlic, peeled and grated

¼ cup rice vinegar

1 tablespoon fresh lime juice

1 tablespoon grape molasses*

2 tablespoons olive oil

2 tablespoons toasted sesame oil

1 teaspoon sea salt

¼ teaspoon freshly ground pepper

The persimmon variety found in Iran is oval and soft inside, whereas the Chinese variety is round and firm, and should be peeled. Persimmons traveled in ancient times from China to Persia via the Silk Road. Iranians love them and eat them as a fruit. I have fond childhood memories of freezing them, taking off the top, and eating the insides like ice cream. We have references to kale, also known as leaf cabbage, both in its curly and flat leaf varieties as far back as the fourth century BCE. It was popular in Europe until the end of the Middle Ages, but it was introduced to Canada by the Russians in the nineteenth century and from there to the U.S. These days, kale has become popular once again, and quite a few varieties are available at supermarkets and farmers markets (it grows well into winter). For this salad, I recommend the more delicate curly leaf variety. Here, I have combine its shredded leaves with the delicious, crunchy, sweet taste of Chinese persimmons (but I also like using Fuji apples, peeled and diced).

1. Place the kale leaves in a salad spinner, cover with water, and add a splash of vinegar. Allow to soak for 10 minutes, then rinse thoroughly. Use the salad spinner to thoroughly dry the kale leaves. Shred the leaves and place them in a large salad bowl.

2. Peel the persimmons, dice into ½ in (1 cm) cubes, and add them to the salad bowl.

3. Place the pumpkin seeds in a wide skillet over medium heat and dry-toast them by shaking the skillet back and forth for a few minutes. Remove from heat and add to the salad bowl.

4. In a small bowl, combine all the ingredients for the dressing. Whisk thoroughly and pour over the salad. Toss well and allow to sit for 10 minutes at room temperature to develop flavor before serving. *Nush-e joon!*

VEGAN

SESAME, NIGELLA + CABBAGE SLAW

salad-e kalam ba siah daneh-o konjed

Serves 6
Prep: 40 minutes

SESAME, NIGELLA + CABBAGE SLAW

"Hot" and "cold" (the Persian version of the yin and yang of food) are perfectly balanced here by combining the "cold" cabbage with the "hot" sesame seeds and nuts. The seeds and nuts also make this a wonderfully nourishing salad for vegetarians.

SALAD

1 lb (450 g) cabbage (any kind), center stalks or core removed

3 curly kale leaves, center stalks removed, shredded

4 Persian cucumbers,* or 1 long seedless cucumber, peeled and thinly sliced

2 large carrots (about 120 g), peeled and shredded

4 spring onions (white and green parts), chopped

SEEDS AND NUTS

¼ cup (40 g) sesame seeds

¼ cup nigella seeds

¼ cup (40 g) coriander seeds

½ cup (170 g) almonds

DRESSING

2 cloves garlic, peeled and grated

½-inch fresh ginger, peeled and grated

1 teaspoon sea salt

½ teaspoon freshly ground pepper

1 tablespoon honey

½ cup rice vinegar

¼ cup (60 ml) olive oil

2 tablespoons toasted sesame oil

1. Place the cabbage and kale leaves in a salad spinner, cover with water, and add a splash of vinegar. Allow to soak for 10 minutes, then rinse thoroughly and use the salad spinner to dry them completely. Shred the leaves, place in a large salad bowl with the remaining salad ingredients, and set aside.

2. Place all the seeds in a wide skillet over medium heat and dry-toast them by shaking the skillet back and forth for a few minutes until the delicious aroma of the seeds rises up. Add the almonds and give the skillet a shake. Transfer the seeds and nuts to the salad bowl.

3. In a saucepan, whisk together all the ingredients for the dressing. Cook over low heat until warm and pour it over the salad. Toss well and adjust seasoning to taste.

4. Serve with plain rice (*kateh*), pasta, bulgur, quinoa, or roast chicken.

Nush-e joon!

___
VARIATION

You can also mix this salad dressing with 1½ lb (680 g) blanched asparagus, broccoli, or French green beans.

V
VEGAN

CARROT + SESAME SALAD

Salad-e havij

Serves 4
Prep: 15 minutes

CARROT + SESAME SALAD

**1½ lb (450 g) carrots,
peeled and julienned
(¼-inch/6 mm)**

DRESSING

**1 clove garlic, peeled and
grated**

**2 tablespoons light soy
sauce**

2 tablespoons rice vinegar

**2 tablespoons toasted
sesame oil**

1 tablespoon honey

**¼ teaspoon red pepper
flakes**

**2 tablespoons sesame seeds,
toasted***

**2 tablespoons chopped fresh
chives or cilantro**

*This is a simple yet delicious salad with a surprisingly wonderful texture
and flavor. The combination of honey, vinegar and sesame oil has been a
part of Persian cooking since ancient times. It makes a great side dish with
rice, bulgur, or quinoa.*

1. In a salad bowl, whisk together all the ingredients for the dressing
and add the carrots, tossing them well in the dressing and adjusting
the seasoning to taste.

GRILLED CORN ON THE COB IN SUMAC SAUCE

balal ba somaq

Serves 4
Prep: 5 minutes
Cooking: 10 minutes

GRILLED CORN ON THE COB + SUMAC SAUCE

DRESSING

1 clove garlic, grated
zest of 2 limes
¼ cup fresh lime juice
½ cup olive oil
1 teaspoon sea salt
½ teaspoon freshly ground
  pepper
2 tablespoons sumac powder
2 tablespoons raw sesame
  seeds
1 teaspoon dried thyme

4 fresh corncobs, husks
  removed

*In Iran, corn on the cob is cooked by street vendors on charcoal braziers and then dipped into salted water. You can choose your own uncooked corn from the street vendor's cart; some people prefer the softer white corn (*shir*) while others choose the tougher yellow corn that is cooked to a crisp, firm bite. Both are delicious. Here, I'm using bi-colored corn and I'm giving you a deliciously flavorful sumac sauce to go with it.*

1. Preheat broiler, or start grill, until very hot.

2. In a small saucepan, mix all the ingredients for the dressing and simmer over low heat for 1 minute. Stir well and remove from heat.

3. Grill the corncobs for about 10 minutes, turning often so the cobs are cooked evenly to a dark golden brown.

4. Remove from the grill, cut if you wish, transfer the corn to a serving bowl and drizzle the dressing on top. Turn in the bowl so the corncobs are well covered with the dressing. *Nush-e joon!*

VEGAN

Serves 6
Prep: 30 minutes, plus chilling
   for 15 minutes
Cooking: 40 minutes

1 lb (450 g) skinless boneless chicken thighs and/or breasts, cut into ½ in (1 cm) strips

1 small onion, peeled and finely chopped

1 teaspoon sea salt

½ teaspoon freshly ground pepper

2 carrots, peeled and chopped

1 cup (150 g) fresh shelled or frozen green peas

4 (3 lb/1.3k g) large Russet potatoes

4 spring onions (white and green parts), chopped

2 celery stalks, chopped

3 medium cucumbers (fresh or pickled), diced

½ cup (40 g) chopped fresh parsley

2 tablespoons chopped fresh tarragon

2/3 cup (115 g) olives, pitted and chopped

3 hard-boiled eggs, peeled and chopped

DRESSING

¾ cup (180 g) thick yogurt or labneh*

2 tablespoons Dijon mustard

¼ cup (60 ml) olive oil

¼ cup (60 ml) rice vinegar

2 tablespoons lime juice

2 teaspoons sea salt

2 teaspoons ground pepper

Belgian chef Lucien Olivier of the Hermitage in Moscow made the original version of this salad back in the 1860s. It was immensely popular and copied all over the world. Iranians quickly adopted it as their own, and most Iranians of my generation have very fond memories of it as one of their favorite dishes, served both at home and in sandwich shops and restaurants. Here, I have replaced the mayonnaise of the original with yogurt and made a short cut for cooking the chicken.

1. Place the chicken strips in a medium-sized pot and add the onion, salt, and pepper. Give the mixture a stir, then cover and cook (no need to add any water) over medium-low heat for 30 minutes. Add the carrots and peas, cover again, and cook for 10 minutes longer. Remove from heat and allow to cool.

2. In a medium saucepan, place the potatoes and cover with water. Bring to a boil, reduce heat to medium and cook for 20 to 30 minutes until potatoes are tender (there should be no resistance when you push a pairing knife through a potato). Peel, dice and set aside.

3. In a large bowl, whisk together all the ingredients for the dressing, or use a blender to mix them.

4. Add the cooked chicken, carrot, and pea mixture to the bowl, together with their juices. Tip in the remaining ingredients and toss well, adjusting the seasoning to taste.

5. Cover the bowl and chill in the fridge for 15 minutes or up to 24 hours (this salad seems to improve with time). Serve with lavash bread, hot pitas, or French bread, and any kind of vegetables or green salad. *Nush-e joon!*

OLIVIER CHICKEN SALAD

salad-e olivieh

EGGPLANT + ZUCCHINI RATATOUILLE

Yatimcheh

Serves 6 to 8
Prep: 20 minutes
Cooking: 1 hour

VEGETABLES

9 Chinese or Japanese eggplants, chopped into 1½ in (4 cm) cubes (about 2½ lb/1.1 kg)

2 zucchini, cut into large dice

1 large green or yellow bell pepper, seeded and chopped

2 large onions, peeled and chopped

2 celery stalks, chopped

4 large tomatoes, peeled* and chopped

1 whole garlic bulb, peeled and chopped

SAUCE

½ cup (60 ml) olive oil

2 teaspoons grape molasses* or honey

1 tablespoon sea salt

1 teaspoon freshly ground pepper

3 bay leaves

1 tablespoon *herbes de Provence* (see note)

GARNISH

¼ cup chopped fresh mint or parsley

Yatimcheh is traditionally made on the stovetop with eggplants, zucchini, onions, garlic, olive oil, salt, pepper, and turmeric. Here, however, I have added tomato (a New World vegetable) and cooked this dish in the oven, with delicious results—much like a Provençal ratatouille. The photo on the facing page shows the vegetables in a rimmed sheet pan, just out of the oven.

1. Preheat oven to 450°F (230°C).

2. Place all the vegetables in a rimmed sheet pan.

3. In a bowl, combine all the ingredients for the sauce and pour this mixture over the vegetables, gently tossing everything together to ensure that the vegetables are completely covered in the sauce.

4. Bake, uncovered, on the central rack in the oven for 30 minutes. Open the oven, pull out the rack, and carefully toss the vegetables again using 2 spatulas. Push back the rack and continue baking for another 30 minutes.

5. Transfer to a serving bowl, and serve hot or at room temperature, as a topping on toasted bread, or as an accompaniment. *Nush-e joon!*

NOTE

If you don't have *herbes de Provence*, you can use a mixture of any fresh or dried and crushed Mediterranean herbs—such as rosemary, thyme, sage, bay leaves, and oregano—according to what you have available.

A soup stall in old Tehran

SOUP

Persian soup or *osh*, is usually a hearty dish—slow-cooked in one pot with beans, fresh herbs and vegetables of the season. It can be made a day in advance to give the flavors a chance to meld, then reheated just before serving. There is a good reason why in Persian, the cook is the "*osh* maker" (*osh paz*), and the kitchen is the "*osh* maker's house" (*osh paz khaneh*). Soup plays an important role in Iranian life, with a special soup for each occasion. Some of my happiest childhood memories revolve around the noodle soup lunches held at our house on Fridays. The ritual would start the day before, with my mother and her helpers making the noodles. Everything was prepared from scratch: beans would be soaked and, armfuls of herbs meticulously washed and chopped. Everyone would lend a hand, cheerfully singing and reciting poetry as they worked. The next day, family and friends would gather together, all seated around the table, young and old alike, each with a bowl of warm, delicious, noodle soup in front of them. I remember those times like yesterday, and I still crave that wonderful sense of togetherness.

Serves 8 to 10
Prep: 20 minutes, plus soaking
  the beans overnight
Cooking: 1 hour

NOODLE + CHICKPEA SOUP

¼ cup (50 g) dried chickpeas

¼ cup (50 g) dried black-eyed peas

1½ cups (300 g) green lentils, rinsed

4 tablespoons vegetable oil

4 large onions, peeled and thinly sliced

10 cloves garlic, peeled and crushed

1 tablespoon sea salt

1 teaspoon freshly ground pepper

2 teaspoons turmeric

3 tablespoons ground cumin

1 tablespoon ground coriander

2 tablespoons ground ginger

12 cups (2.8 l) water

2 cups liquid kashk* or buttermilk

1 tablespoon grape molasses

12 oz (340 g) dried Persian noodles or fettuccine

3 tablespoons dried mint

1 cup (85 g) coarsely chopped fresh chives or (100 g) spring onions (white and green parts)

1 cup (85 g) chopped fresh dill weed

2 cups (170 g) chopped fresh parsley

2 lb (900 g) chopped fresh spinach, or 1 lb (450 g) frozen chopped spinach

In Iran, it is said that eating noodles brings good fortune, that is why noodle soup is always served on Nowruz, the Iranian New Year's Day.

1. Place chickpeas, black-eyed peas, and lentils in a large bowl, cover with water 2 in (5 cm) above the chickpeas and allow to soak overnight. Drain, rinse, and set aside.

2. In a very large pot, heat the oil over medium heat. Add the onions and garlic, and sauté, stirring occasionally, for 15 minutes, or until golden brown. Add the salt, pepper, turmeric, cumin, coriander, ginger, and chickpea, black-eyed pea and lentil mixture, and stir-fry for 1 minute.

3. Add 12 cups of water and bring to a boil. Reduce the heat to medium, cover, and simmer for 30 minutes, or until chickpeas are tender.

4. Add the kashk. Use a handheld mixer to partially purée the ingredients in the soup.

5. Add the noodles and cook for 5 minutes, stirring occasionally.

6. Add the herbs and spinach and continue cooking, stirring occasionally, for another 10 minutes.

7. Adjust the seasoning to taste and pour the soup into a tureen or individual serving bowls. *Nush-e joon!*

NOODLE +CHICKPEA SOUP

osh-e reshteh

POMEGRANATE
SOUP

osh-e anar

Serves 6–8
Prep: 20 minutes
Cooking: 1 hour

½ cup (100 g) dried mung beans

¼ cup (50 g) barley

¼ cup (50 g) lentils

4 tablespoons olive oil

4 medium onions, peeled and thinly sliced

8 cloves garlic, peeled and sliced

1 large beet, peeled and chopped

1 tablespoon sea salt

1 teaspoon freshly ground pepper

2 teaspoons turmeric

1 teaspoon ground cinnamon

1 tablespoon advieh (Persian spice mix)*

8 cups (1.9 l) water

2 bottles (945 ml) pomegranate juice

¼ cup (50 g) rice

2 cups (170 g) chopped fresh parsley

2 cups (170 g) chopped fresh cilantro

2 cups (170 g) chopped fresh mint

2 cups (200 g) chopped spring onions (white and green parts)

2 tablespoons ground golpar*

GARNISH

2 tablespoons chopped fresh dill weed

1 cup (150 g) pomegranate arils

For best results, make your soup a day in advance to give the flavors a chance to meld; reheat it just before serving. Add the garnish at the last minute, after pouring the soup into the tureen.

1. Place the mung beans, lentils and barley in a container and cover with water 2 in (5 cm) above the beans. Soak overnight. Drain and set aside.

2. Heat the oil in a large, heavy-bottomed over medium heat. Add the onions and garlic and sauté, stirring occasionally, for 10 minutes, or until lightly golden brown.

3. Add the beans barley and lentil mixture, and the beets, salt, pepper, turmeric, cinnamon, and advieh, and sauté for 1 minute. Pour in the water and bring to a boil. Reduce heat to medium-low, cover, and simmer for 25 minutes, stirring occasionally to prevent sticking.

4. Add the pomegranate juice, rice, herbs, and bring back to a boil. Cover again and continue to simmer over medium-low heat for 20 minutes, or until the beans are tender. Use a handheld mixer to partially purée the soup.

5. Add the golpar and give it a stir. Cook, uncovered, over medium heat for 5 minutes. Adjust seasoning to taste: the flavor should be sweet and sour—if too sweet, add a squeeze or two of lime. Cover and keep warm until ready to serve.

6. Pour the soup into a tureen and garnish. Stir in the garnish just before ladling soup into individual bowls. *Nush-e joon!*

Makes 6 to 8 servings
Prep: 20 minutes
Cooking: 1 hour

SOUP

½ cup olive oil

1 onion, peeled and thinly sliced

2 cloves garlic, peeled and thinly sliced

1 carrot, peeled and roughly chopped

3 leeks (white and green parts), washed thoroughly and finely chopped

1 kohlrabi or turnip (about 1/2lb/225g), peeled and roughly chopped

½ cup (100 g) barley

¼ cup (50 g) mung beans

1 teaspoon sea salt

½ teaspoon freshly ground pepper

CHASHNI (SAVORY)

1 cup kashk, sour cream or almond milk

2 tablespoons fresh lime juice

1 teaspoon grape molasses or honey

GARNISH

½ cup (40 g) chopped fresh parsley or 3 tbs dried

½ cup (40 g) chopped fresh cilantro or 3 tbs dried

½ cup (40 g) chopped fresh dill weed or 3 tbs dried

½ cup (40 g) chopped fresh tarragon or 3 tbs dried

This is one of the oldest and tastiest of the Persian soups—I often make it at home. For a vegan option replace the kashk with almond milk to have it dairy-free. Chashni is a savory souring agent, that is added to a dish to enhance the flavor—a sort of Persian umami, you might say. For non-vegetarians, you can replace the water with 8 cups (1.9 liters) chicken broth.

1 Heat the oil in a large, heavy-bottomed pot over medium heat. Add all the ingredients for the soup and sauté for 5 minutes. Add 10 cups of water and bring to a boil. Reduce heat to medium-low, cover and simmer for 45 minutes, or until the beans are tender.

2. Use a handheld mixer to partially purée the soup.

3. To temper the kashk: In a small bowl, mix together the kashk, lime juice, and grape molasses with a few spoonfuls of the soup, then pour it into the pot with the rest of the soup and stir well. Cover and continue to simmer over a medium-low heat for 10 minutes. Keep warm until ready to serve.

4. Just before serving, add the herbs for the garnish and stir the soup well. Adjust the seasoning to taste, adding more salt, pepper, or lime juice if needed.

5. Pour soup into a tureen and serve with flat bread. *Nush-e joon!*

BARLEY +LEEK SOUP

osh-e jow

Serves 4
Prep: 20 minutes
Cooking: 1 hour

GINGER + TURMERIC CHICKEN SOUP

2 lb (900 g) skinless chicken legs and thighs

6 cups (1.5 liters) water

1 onion, peeled and quartered

4 cloves garlic, peeled and crushed

1 large carrot, peeled and chopped

1 large celery stalk, chopped

1 medium turnip, peeled and chopped

1 Russet potato (about ½ lb/225 g), peeled and quartered

2 teaspoons sea salt

½ teaspoon freshly ground pepper

1 in (2.5 cm) fresh ginger root, peeled and grated

1 in (2.5 cm) fresh turmeric root,* peeled and grated, or ½ teaspoon ground turmeric

2 bay leaves

GARNISH

¼ cup (20 g) fresh chopped cilantro, or parsley

1 fresh lime

Everyone should know how to make a simple chicken soup. This is an excellent recipe, made with turnip, cilantro, ginger, and turmeric—suitable for any occasion, but especially good if you are feeling a little under the weather. My mother used to make it for me and my sisters and now my husband makes it for me when I'm not feeling well.

1. Heat a medium-sized, heavy-bottomed pot over medium-high heat (no oil is needed) and sear the chicken on all sides until browned.

2. Pour in the water and bring to a boil, skimming away the froth as it forms.

3. Add the rest of the ingredients to the broth and bring back to a boil. Reduce heat to medium, cover and cook for 1 hour.

4. Just before serving, remove the bay leaves. Add the cilantro and a squeeze or two of lime juice, and give the soup a good stir. Adjust the seasoning to taste, adding more salt, pepper, or lime juice if needed.

5. Serve with good fresh bread (and butter). *Nush-e joon!*

GINGER + TURMERIC CHICKEN SOUP

sup-e morgh-o zanjebil

Chicken and duck eggs in
Rasht, by the Caspian Sea.

EGGS + KUKUS

Iranians love eggs, whatever way they are cooked, but they are especially fond of kuku, a type of open-faced omelet similar to the Italian frittata and the Arab *eggah*. Filled with vegetables and herbs, a good kuku should be thick and rather fluffy. A frittata pan, consisting of two interlinking pans that fit one on top of the other, is perfect for making the kukus in this book—a regular pan will also be fine; you will just have to cook the top under the broiler for a couple of minutes. I am giving you several techniques for making kuku: on the stovetop, in the oven using a quarter-sized rimmed sheet pan lined with parchment paper, and a combination of the two using an iron skillet. Try them and use the technique that works for you. One of the best things about kukus is that they can be eaten hot or at room temperature, and they keep very well in the fridge for up to 4 days.

People who don't cook are prone to say, "I can cook an egg and that's about it." Actually, to cook a perfect egg does take practice. Below, I've given a few tips that might help, but to get it just right for your taste, you may have to experiment a little. Each recipe is for 2 eggs; if you're cooking more than a couple of eggs, you'll need a bigger pan in each case.

BOILED EGGS

1. Place the eggs in a small saucepan, cover with water, and bring to a boil. Immediately turn off the heat.

2. Cover and let the pot stand—4 minutes for soft-boiled eggs, 7 minutes for medium-boiled, and 10 minutes for hard-boiled. (These times are for sea level; in mountainous regions, the times need to be considerably increased, depending on the altitude.)

3. Drain the cooking water and vigorously shake the saucepan to crack the eggs. Cover with cold water to stop any further cooking.

4. Peel the eggs and serve with salt and pepper, your favorite bread, and butter. *Nush-e joon!*

POACHED EGGS

1. Fill a wide skillet with water. Add 2 teaspoons vinegar and a pinch of salt and bring to a boil.

2. Break each egg into a small cup and slip it into the boiling water, one after the other. Reduce heat to low, cover and allow to simmer for 3 to 6 minutes (depending on how you like your eggs, from runny to firm).

3. Remove each egg with a slotted spoon or spider and shake gently to ensure all the water drips off. Serve on top of your favorite toasted bread—or on a bed of rice, pasta, quinoa, or salad—sprinkled with a little salt and freshly ground pepper.

FRIED EGGS

1. Heat an 8in (20cm) skillet over medium heat and add 2 tablespoons olive oil and 1 table-spoon butter. When the oil starts to sizzle, gently break each egg into the skillet.

2. Sprinkle with salt and freshly ground pepper, cover, and cook for 4 minutes, or until the whites are softly set and the yolks done to your taste. Alternatively, cook the eggs for 1 minute, or until the whites begin to set, then tilt the skillet and spoon the hot oil in the pan around and over the yolks until they are cooked to your taste, from runny to firm.

3. Serve on toasted flat bread, my favorite is the Persian barbari, with Yogurt and Persian Shallot Dip (mast-o musir, see page 49) .

VE
VEGETARIAN

POACHED EGGS WITH SHALLOT + YOGURT

tokhm-e morgh-e ab paz

TOMATO, CUMIN + SWEET PEPPER OMELET

omlet

Makes 4 omelets
Prep: 15 minutes
Cooking: 10 minutes

TOMATO, CUMIN + SWEET PEPPER OMELET

The aroma and flavor of cumin bring out the taste of this tomato and bell pepper omelet. Served with fresh, hot lavash bread, this was one of my favorite dishes when I was growing up in Iran. Traditionally, for making this omelet, after all the ingredients have been sautéed in a large skillet, the eggs would be broken on top and cooked over low heat until firm. Here, however, I'm showing you how to make individual omelets.

BATTER

4 eggs
2 tablespoons milk
¼ teaspoon sea salt

FILLING

2 tablespoons olive oil
1 teaspoon cumin seeds
1 medium onion, peeled
  and sliced
½ red bell pepper, seeded
  and chopped
2 cloves garlic, peeled and
  crushed
2 medium tomatoes,
  peeled* and diced
½ teaspoon sea salt
¼ teaspoon freshly
  ground pepper
¼ cup (20 g) shredded
  fresh basil

4 teaspoons olive oil for
  cooking the omelets

GARNISH

1 cup (85 g) fresh basil
  leaves

1. To make the batter: Break the eggs into a mixing bowl, add the milk and salt, and whisk for 20 seconds (about 20 strokes of the whisk).

2. To make the filling: Heat the 2 tablespoons oil in a medium-sized skillet over medium heat, add the cumin, onion, and bell pepper and stir-fry for 1 minute, or until the onion becomes translucent. Add the garlic and stir-fry for 1 minute longer.

3. Add the remaining ingredients for the filling and stir-fry for another minute. Remove from heat and set aside.

4. To make an individual omelet: Heat 1 teaspoon of the oil in an 8 in (20 cm) non-stick omelet pan or skillet set over medium heat, until very hot but not smoking.

5. Pour a thin layer of the egg mixture into the pan (about 2 tablespoons). Lift and tilt the pan in different directions, so that the base is coated in an even layer of batter.

6. Once the egg has set, place 2 tablespoons of filling in the center. Use a rubber spatula to loosen the edges of the omelet and fold over. Tilt the pan and roll or slide the omelet out onto an individual plate. Continue until you have made all the omelets.

7. Serve hot with lavash bread and fresh basil. *Nush-e joon!*

Serves 4
Prep: 10 minutes
Cooking: 30 minutes (if using
  a gas flame for eggplants)

EGGPLANT + EGG SPREAD

EGGPLANT
2–3 large eggplants
  (about 2½ lb/1.1 kg)
½ cup (120 ml) olive oil
5 cloves garlic, peeled and
  thinly sliced
2 teaspoons sea salt
½ teaspoon freshly ground
  pepper
1 teaspoon turmeric
4 eggs

GARNISH
1 cup (85 g) fresh basil leaves
½ cup (120 g) plain yogurt

Mirza qasemi is made throughout the Caspian region, but each town has its own variation: some people add tomato; others cook the eggs and eggplants separately and mix them together at the end. But the result is always a deliciously smoky taste. Here I have spread the eggplant on a piece of flat bread with a fried egg on top.

1. Roast the eggplants on all sides over a cooktop flame until the skin is burnt and completely blackened. If you don't have a gas cooktop, preheat the oven to 450°F (230°C). Prick the eggplants in several places with a fork to prevent them from bursting during cooking. Place them on a rack in a rimmed sheet pan and bake in the oven for 1 hour.

2. Place the eggplants on a chopping board and leave until cool enough to handle. Then use your hands to remove and discard the skins. Finely chop the eggplants.

3. Heat the oil in a wide, deep skillet over medium heat and sauté the garlic for 1 to 2 minutes, or until golden. Add the salt, pepper, turmeric, and chopped eggplants, and sauté for 5 to 10 minutes, or until all the juices have been absorbed.

4. Reduce heat to low and spread out the eggplant mixture evenly in the skillet. Break the eggs on top. Cook over low heat for 15 to 20 minutes, or until the eggs are softly set.

5. Stir the mixture gently with a wooden spoon, then transfer to a serving platter. Garnish with fresh basil and yogurt, and serve with toasted bread. *Nush-e joon!*

VE
VEGETARIAN

EGGPLANT +
EGG SPREAD

mirza qasemi

Serves 4
Prep: 30 minutes
Cooking: 40 minutes

Perfect in summer when squash is in season, this is one of the easiest kukus to prepare. I made the one in the photo using young squash from our local farmers' market, mixing it with onion, garlic, and fresh mint. It was light, fluffy, and delicious. After the shoot, four of us ate it with the crispy lavash and a dollop of the yogurt. You can also replace the squash with young, tender, Chinese eggplants (contrary to squash, eggplants should always be peeled but because Chinese eggplants are sweet, there is no need to soak in salt water to remove bitterness).

5 to 6 zucchini (about
   1½ lb/680 g)
½ cup (120 ml) olive oil
2 large onions, peeled and
   thinly sliced
4 cloves garlic, peeled and
   thinly sliced
4 eggs
1 cup (85 g) chopped fresh
   parsley or mint
1½ teaspoons sea salt
½ teaspoon freshly ground
   pepper
1 teaspoon turmeric
½ teaspoon red pepper
   flakes
1 teaspoon baking powder
1 tablespoon rice flour
1 tablespoon fresh plain
   bread crumbs
Zest of 1 lime

GARNISH
1 cup (85 g) fresh basil leaves

1. Wash the zucchini and thoroughly pat dry before slicing thinly (a mandolin is a useful tool for this, but be very careful not to cut your fingers).

2. In a wide skillet, heat 2 tablespoons of the oil over medium-high heat. Add the onions, garlic, and sliced zucchini, and stir-fry for 5 minutes, or until translucent. Remove from heat and allow to cool completely.

3. Break the eggs into a large mixing bowl. Add the remaining ingredients and beat lightly with a fork. Add the zucchini mixture and fold in gently using a rubber spatula (taking care not to over-mix).

4. Heat the remaining oil in a 10 in (25 cm) skillet (or frittata pan) over medium-low heat, until hot but not smoking. Pour in the kuku mixture, and cook, covered, for 15 to 20 minutes, or until it has set. If you are using a frittata pan, simply flip over and cook the other side for another 15 to 20 minutes, or until golden. If not, cook the top under a hot broiler for 1 to 2 minutes until a tester comes out clean.

5. Cut the kuku into wedges, garnish fresh basil and serve with Yogurt and Persian Shallot Dip (mast-o musir, see page 49), hot or at room temperature with bread. *Nush-e joon!*

VARIATION

Eggplant Kuku

Follow the main recipe, replacing the zucchini with 8 Chinese eggplants (about 2½ lb/1.1 kg), peeled and thinly sliced, and the red pepper flakes with 1 tablespoon fresh lime juice.

SUMMER SQUASH KUKU

kuku-ye kadu sabz

Makes 6 servings
Preparation time: 45 minutes
Cooking time: 15 minutes.

CARAMELIZING ONIONS
4 tablespoons olive oil
2 medium, yellow onions, peeled and finely chopped

GARNISH
1 tablespoon olive oil
½ cup (75 g) dried barberries, soaked in cold water for 15 minutes, rinsed, and drained
1 teaspoon grape molasses* or sugar
2 tablespoons water

BATTER
7 eggs
1 teaspoon baking powder
1 tablespoon advieh (Persian spice mix)*
1½ teaspoons sea salt
1 teaspoon freshly ground black pepper
½ teaspoon turmeric
2 cloves garlic, peeled and finely chopped
½ cup (40 g) finely chopped Romaine lettuce
½ cup (50 g) finely chopped spring onions (white and green parts)
1 cup (85 g) finely chopped fresh parsley
1 cup (85 g) finely chopped fresh cilantro
1 cup (85 g) finely chopped fresh dill weed
1 tablespoon dried fenugreek leaves (not seeds)
½ cup (60 g) coarsely chopped walnuts
1 tablespoon rice flour
2 tablespoons olive oil

FRESH HERB KUKU

This kuku brings back golden memories of my childhood in Iran. On the eve of the Persian New Year, our kitchen would be buzzing with activity as my mother and other members of the family were busy preparing kuku sabzi, *an essential dish for the New Year feast. The tantalizing aroma of the herbs floating around the house would drive us children crazy with the desire to have some of the kuku—but we had to wait until the festivities began.*

The key to making this kuku is to thoroughly wash and dry the herbs before chopping them (see page 20).

1. To caramelize the onions: Heat the oil in a wide skillet over medium heat and sauté the onions for 10 to 15 minutes, or until lightly golden. Remove the onions and allow to cool.

2. To make the garnish: In the same skillet, place the oil, barberries, grape molasses, and the water, and stir-fry for 4 minutes over medium heat (taking care as barberries burn easily). Transfer the barberries to a small bowl and set aside.

3. Preheat the oven to 400°F (200°C) and line a *quarter-sized (9½ x 13 in/ 24 x 33 cm) rimmed sheet pan* with parchment paper.

4. To make the batter: Break the eggs into a large mixing bowl. Add the baking powder, advieh, salt, pepper, and turmeric. Beat lightly with a fork. Add the garlic, lettuce, herbs, walnuts, flour, caramelized onions, and oil, and fold in gently using a rubber spatula (do not over-mix).

5. To cook the kuku: Paint the lined sheet pan with oil. Pour in the batter, and gently shake the pan to even out the batter. Bake in the preheated oven for 15 minutes.

6. Remove from the oven and place on a cooling rack. Garnish with the caramelized barberries. Cut the kuku into pieces according to your fancy. Serve hot, or at room temperature, with lavash bread and Yogurt and Persian Shallot Dip (*mast-o musir*, page 49). *Nush-e joon!*

FRESH HERB KUKU
kuku sabzi

Serves 6
Prep: 20 minutes
Cooking: 20 minutes.

CAULIFLOWER KUKU

½ cup (120 ml) olive oil

1 medium onion, peeled and thinly sliced

2 cloves garlic, peeled and finely chopped

1 small head cauliflower, cut up into florets and coarsely chopped

1½ teaspoons sea salt

½ teaspoon freshly ground pepper

1 teaspoon ground cumin

¼ teaspoon turmeric

¼ teaspoon cayenne

½ cup (40 g) chopped fresh parsley

4 eggs

½ teaspoon baking powder

1 tablespoon rice flour or potato starch

½ cup (100 g) goat-milk cheese, crumbled

For this recipe, everything is cooked together in one skillet and finished in the oven. This is a simpler process than for the Summer Squash Kuku where the vegetables are cooked separately and then mixed with the eggs, cooked on the stove-top, and flipped over.

1. Preheat the oven to 400°F (200°C).

2. Heat ¼ cup of oil in a medium-sized, ovenproof skillet over medium heat. Add the onion, garlic, cauliflower, salt, pepper, cumin, turmeric, cayenne, and parsley, and stir-fry for 4 to 5 minutes, or until the cauliflower is soft.

3. Meanwhile, break the eggs into a mixing bowl, add the remaining ingredients and whisk lightly.

4. Pour the kuku mixture into the skillet and give it a quick stir using a rubber spatula. Reduce heat to low, flatten the surface of the kuku, and pour the remaining oil around the edges. Cook for 4 minutes.

5. Transfer the skillet to the preheated oven and bake for 8 to 10 minutes, or until the edges are lightly browned and coming away from the skillet.

6. Remove the skillet from the oven, cut into wedges, and serve with bread, fresh herbs, and yogurt. *Nush-e joon!*

CAULIFLOWER KUKU

kuku-ye gol-e kalam

Pizza with Caspian-style topping,
made in an iron skillet (page 123).

MEATBALLS, PASTA + PIZZA

This section is a catchall for some of my favorite childhood dishes from Iran. Turnovers, called sanbuseh in Persian (samosa in India), were much more popular in the 10th century than they have been in recent years, but they are having a comeback. ✑ Meatballs are very popular in northeastern Iran, where the Tabrizis make some magnificent ones. As well as being easy to prepare, my own are made with lots of fresh herbs, really adding to the overall flavor, and served with a delicious sauce or glaze. I have also included a popular type of patty called *shami* usually made with ground lamb, which I have replaced with quinoa. ✑ Most people associate pasta with Italy, and understandably so, but Iranians were pasta eaters long before the Italians. So I have included a favorite pasta dish in remembrance of how durum wheat was introduced by the ancient Iranians to China and later, via the Arabs, to Italy. ✑ The name for pizza derives from the Italian pronunciation of "pitta," which is what the ancient Greeks used to call flat breads from Turkey and Iran. Here I've given you an easy-to-make skillet pizza topped with a wonderful combination of walnut, pomegranate, olive, oregano, and golpar—a Caspian specialty.

FAVA BEAN + DILL MEATBALLS

kufteh baqali

Makes 16 meatballs
Prep: 45 minutes,
Cooking: 25 minutes

MEATBALLS

½ cup (100 g) rice

6 cups (1.4 l) water

8 oz (225 g) skinned* fresh or frozen fava beans (see note)

1 small onion, peeled and grated

4 cloves garlic, grated

3 cups (250 g) chopped fresh dill weed

2 teaspoons fine sea salt

1 teaspoon ground pepper

1 teaspoon turmeric

1 tablespoon ground cumin

3 eggs, lightly beaten

1 lb (450 g) ground turkey thigh or lamb

½ cup (75 g) rice flour

TOMATO SAUCE

¼ cup (60 ml) olive oil

2 onions, peeled and thinly sliced

2 teaspoons fine sea salt

½ teaspoon freshly ground pepper

½ teaspoon turmeric

½ teaspoon red pepper flakes

3 cups peeled, fresh or canned (28 oz/825 ml) tomato purée

2 cups water

NOTE

If using fresh fava beans in their pods, you'll need 1½ lb (680 g) to get 8 oz (225 g) shelled and skinned beans. Frozen skinned fava beans are available from Iranian markets, or you can use lima beans or edamame instead.

FAVA BEAN + DILL MEATBALLS

1. *To make the meatballs:* Place the rice and water in a medium-sized saucepan and bring to a boil. Reduce heat to medium and cook for 5 minutes. Add the fava beans, and cook for another 5 minutes. Drain, *do not rinse*, and allow to cool completely.

2. In a large mixing bowl, combine together all the ingredients for meatballs with fava and rice mixture.

3. Knead lightly until the mixture has the consistency of a smooth paste (do not over-mix). Cover and chill for 10 minutes (or up to 24 hours) in the fridge.

4. *Meanwhile, to make the tomato sauce*: In a large, heavy-based pot, heat the oil over medium heat and sauté the onions for 10 to 15 minutes, or until golden. Add the remaining ingredients for the sauce and bring to a boil. Reduce heat to medium-low, cover, and allow to simmer for 5 minutes.

5. Preheat the oven to 450°F (230°C). Generously oil a wide, non-reactive baking dish, large enough to fit 16 meatballs, (about 12 x 14 in/30 x 35 cm). Shape the meat paste into 16 balls, each the size of large walnuts. Gently arrange them in baking dish and brush with oil. Bake in the oven for 10 minutes.

6. Pull out the oven rack and gently pour the hot tomato sauce over the meatballs. Cover with an oiled sheet of parchment paper and continue to bake for 7 minutes longer. Keep warm until ready to serve.

7. Serve with Yogurt and Persian Shallot Dip (*mast-o musir*, page 49) and bread.
Nush-e joon!

VEGETARIAN VARIATION

For a vegetarian version, replace the turkey with cooked quinoa. To cook the quinoa: Place 2 cups quinoa (rinsed thoroughly) and 3 cups water in a medium saucepan, stir gently and bring to a boil. Reduce heat to low, cover and cook for 20 minutes. Remove from heat and allow to cool. In step 2, place all the ingredients for the meatballs and the cooked quinoa in a food processor and pulse until you have a grainy paste.

VEO
VEGETARIAN
OPTION

Makes: 24–30 meatballs
Prep: 20 minutes plus 10
    minutes of refrigeration
Cooking: 20 minutes

MEATBALLS

1 large onion, peeled and
    quartered
1½ cups (180 g) raw pistachio
    kernels (see note)
½ cup (15 g) fresh plain
    bread crumbs
3 cups (250 g) chopped fresh
    parsley
1 cup (85 g) chopped fresh
    tarragon
1 cup (85 g) chopped fresh
    cilantro
1 tablespoon fresh lime juice
1 teaspoon red pepper flakes
1 teaspoon freshly ground
    black pepper
1 tablespoon ground cumin
2 teaspoons sea salt
2 lb (900 g) ground turkey
    thighs, lamb, or deboned
    fish fillets
1 egg

½ cup oil to brush meatballs

GLAZE

1 cup (240 ml) pomegranate
    molasses*
1/3 cup (80 ml) grape
    molasses*
1 teaspoon salt
½ teaspoon freshly ground
    pepper
½ teaspoon red pepper
    flakes

GARNISH

1 cup (150 g) pomegranate arils

PISTACHIO + POMEGRANATE MEATBALLS

*Years ago I was inspired by a sixteenth-century Persian cookbook to create
this recipe and combine a mixture of pomegranate and grape molasses
for the sauce. To my surprise, last year in Kerman, where they have the best
of both pomegranates and pistachios, a local cook served me pistachio
meatballs with a pomegranate sauce.*

1. To make the meatballs: Place all the ingredients, except the ground
turkey and egg, in a food processor and pulse until you have a grainy
paste. Transfer to a large mixing bowl and add the turkey and egg.
Lightly knead with your hands for a few minutes (do not over-mix).
Cover and chill in the fridge for at least 10 minutes or up to 24 hours.

2. Preheat the oven to 450°F (230°C). Generously oil a wide,
non-reactive baking dish, large enough to fit 24 meatballs,
(about 12 x 14 in/30 x 35 cm) and set aside.

3. Remove the turkey paste from the fridge and shape into walnut-
sized balls (about 1½ tablespoons each) using an ice-cream scoop.
Place the meatballs in the baking dish and brush well with oil. Bake in
the oven for 5 to 15 minute (depending on your oven).

4. Meanwhile, in another mixing bowl, combine all the ingredients for
the glaze.

5. Spoon the glaze over the meatballs and bake for another 5 minutes
to infuse them with the flavor of pomegranate.

6. Garnish with the pomegranate arils and serve warm with the sauce.
Nush-e joon!

VEGETARIAN VARIATION

For a vegetarian version, in step 1, replace the meat with cooked quinoa. To cook
the quinoa: Place 2 cups quinoa (rinsed thoroughly) and 3 cups water in a
medium saucepan, stir gently and bring to a boil. Reduce heat to low, cover and
cook for 20 minutes. In step 1, place all the ingredients for the meatballs,
increasing number of eggs to 3, and the cooked quinoa in a food processor and
pulse until you have a grainy paste.

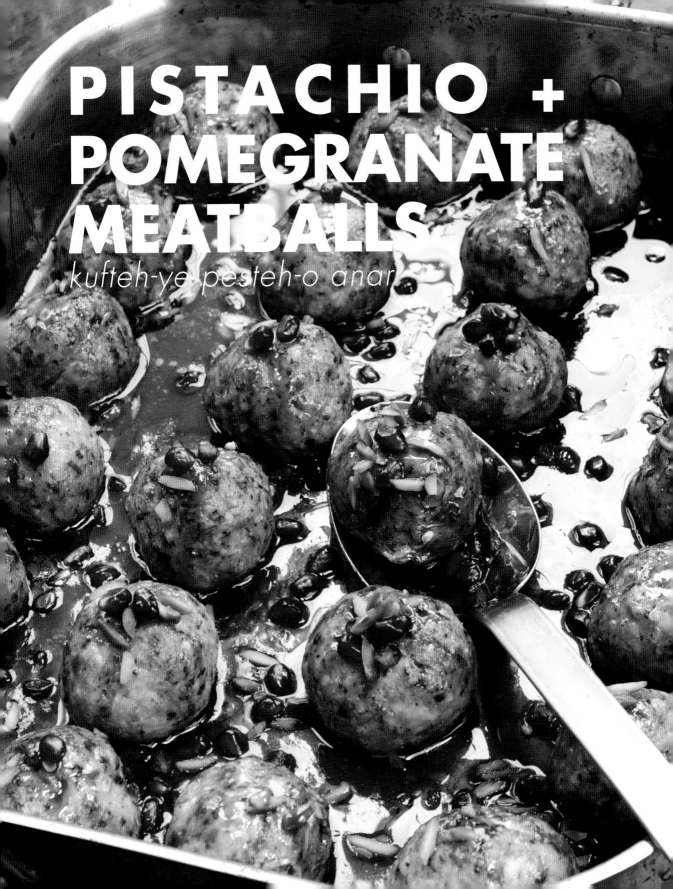

PISTACHIO + POMEGRANATE MEATBALLS

kufteh-ye pesteh-o anar

CHICKPEA MEATBALLS

gondi

Makes 12 meatballs/Serves 6
Prep: 20 minutes, plus chilling
  for 30 minutes
Cooking: 45 minutes

CHICKPEA MEATBALLS / GONDI

MEATBALLS
2 medium onions, peeled
  and grated
1 lb (450 g) ground chicken
  thigh meat
1 teaspoon sea salt
½ teaspoon freshly ground
  pepper
1 teaspoon ground
  cardamom
½ teaspoon ground saffron
  dissolved in 2 tablespoons
  rose water*
2 tablespoons water

½ cup (50 g) chickpea flour

BROTH
2 tablespoons olive oil
1 large onion, peeled and
  thinly sliced
1½ teaspoons sea salt
½ teaspoon freshly ground
  pepper
½ teaspoon turmeric
3½ cups (830 ml) water

SWEET AND SOUR SYRUP
½ cup (120 ml) wine vinegar
3 tablespoons grape
  molasses* or brown sugar
1 teaspoon dried mint

GARNISH
¼ cup (20 g) chopped fresh
  cilantro or mint

Gondi is popular among the Jewish community of Iran, especially for Shabbat. Some say the name is from one of two villages of the same name in Iran.

1. To make the meatballs: In a mixing bowl, combine the onions, ground chicken, salt, pepper, cardamom, saffron-infused rose water, and 2 tablespoons water. Knead the mixture lightly with your hands.

2. Add the chickpea flour, a little at a time, and continue to knead until all the flour has been absorbed (do not over-mix, it will make the meatballs dense). Cover and chill in the fridge for at least 30 minutes or up to 24 hours.

3. To make the broth: Heat the oil in a medium-sized pot over medium heat and sauté the onions for 10 to 15 minutes, or until golden brown. Add the salt, pepper, and turmeric, and stir-fry for 1 minute. Pour in the water and bring to a boil.

4. Shape the paste into walnut-sized balls (using an ice cream scoop) and gently add them, one by one, to the broth. Bring back to a boil. Reduce heat to medium and simmer, uncovered, for 30 minutes.

5. In a small bowl, combine the vinegar, grape molasses, and mint, and pour over the meatballs. Continue to cook over medium heat for another 15 minutes.

6. Adjust the seasoning to taste, then cover and keep warm. Just before serving, garnish with the cilantro. *Nush-e joon!*

SWEET + SOUR CHICKPEA PATTIES

shami-e-ard-e nokhodchi

Makes 16 patties/Serves 4
Prep: 30 minutes, plus chilling
  for 15 minutes
Cooking: 20 minutes

SWEET + SOUR CHICKPEA PATTIES

PATTIES
2 cups (12.6 oz, 360 g)
  quinoa, thoroughly rinsed
1 small onion, peeled and
  quartered
1 teaspoon sea salt
1 teaspoon freshly ground
  pepper
½ teaspoon turmeric
½ teaspoon ground saffron
  threads
3 eggs
1¼ cups (125 g) chickpea
  flour, sifted

½ cup (120 ml) olive oil, for
  frying

SWEET AND SOUR GLAZE
2 tablespoons olive oil
1 onion, peeled and thinly
  sliced
1 teaspoon salt
½ teaspoon freshly ground
  black pepper
1 teaspoon turmeric
2 teaspoons dried mint
½ cup (120 ml) water
½ cup (120 ml) wine vinegar
¼ cup (120 ml) grape
  molasses*

GARNISH
Fresh basil, mint, tarragon,
  radishes, spring onions

These patties are traditionally made with lamb, but here I am giving you a deliciously vegetarian version using quinoa.

1. ***To cook the quinoa:*** Place the quinoa and 3 cups water in a medium saucepan, stir gently and bring to a boil. Reduce heat to low, cover and cook for 20 minutes Remove from heat and allow to cool.

2. ***To make the patties:*** In a food processor place the cooked quinoa and all the ingredients for the patties, and pulse until you have a thick, soft paste (add more chickpea flour if necessary). Cover and chill in the fridge for 15 minutes or up to 24 hours.

3. In a wide skillet, heat 2 tablespoons oil over medium-low heat, until hot but not smoking. Place a bowl of warm water next to your cooking area.

4. Scoop the paste (using an ice-cream scoop) into lumps each the size of a walnut. Dip your hands in the warm water and flatten each lump between your damp palms into a round shape, 2½ to 3 inches (6 to 8 cm) across, making a hole in the center with your finger.

5. Fry the patties on each side for about 2 to 3 minutes, until golden brown, adding more oil if necessary. Remove the patties gently with an offset spatula, place on a plate, and set aside.

6. ***To make the glaze:*** Heat the oil in the same skillet over medium heat. Add the onion and sauté for 10 to 15 minutes, until golden brown. Add the salt, pepper, turmeric and mint, and stir-fry for 20 seconds. Pour in the water, vinegar, and grape molasses, and bring to a boil. Reduce heat to low and simmer for 5 to 10 minutes, until you have a thick syrup.

7. Carefully arrange the patties in the glaze and allow to simmer over low heat for 5 to 10 minutes, until they have absorbed some of the glaze. Keep warm until ready to serve.

8. Garnish, according to your fancy, with fresh herbs, radishes, and/or spring onions, and serve with bread, pickles, or salad. *Nush-e joon!*

Makes: 25 pieces
Prep: 30 minutes plus 1 hour for
  dough to thaw
Cooking: 35 minutes

DOUGH

3 packs ready-made frozen
  puff pastry, thawed for 1
  hour

FILLING

2 tablespoons olive oil,

1 onion, peeled and thinly
  sliced

2 cloves garlic, peeled and
  chopped

2 tablespoons water

1 lb (450 g) ground lamb or
  chicken thighs

1 teaspoon cayenne

2 teaspoons sea salt

1 teaspoon ground pepper

½ teaspoon turmeric

1 teaspoon cinnamon

2 teaspoons ground cumin

1 cup (85 g) pistachio
  kernels, ground

1 cup (85 g) chopped
  fresh mint leaves or
  1 tablespoon dried

2 cups (170 g) chopped fresh
  parsley

1 cup (85 g) chopped fresh
  tarragon leaves or
  1 tablespoon dried

EGG WASH

2 egg yolks, lightly beaten
  with 2 tablespoons milk

DUSTING

½ cup confectioners' sugar
  mixed with 2 tablespoons
  dried crushed rose petals
  and 4 tablespoons ground
  pistachio kernels

It was a 17th-century Iranian court cookbook that inspired me to develop this recipe. Each turnover is salty and savory inside, while the outside has a sweet and aromatic dusting of confectioner's sugar, rose petals, and ground pistachios. Here, I am using a ready-made frozen puff pastry, which makes it easy and the result is equally delicious.

1. To prepare the filling: In a large skillet, place the oil, onion, garlic, 2 tablespoons water, and lamb, cover and cook over low heat for 15 minutes. Add the rest of the ingredients for the filling and sauté over medium heat for 5 to 10 minutes until the filling is completely dry. Remove from heat and allow to cool.

2. Heat the oven to 350°F (180°C). Line a few sheet pans with parchment paper.

3. On a cool, floured surface, unfold one package of the dough. Cut the dough into 3-inch circles, using a cookie cutter (or the open end of a glass) dipped in flour. Fill each circle with 2 full-teaspoons of the filling. Fold each circle into a crescent shape and seal. Fold over the edges using your fingers and pinch to double seal. Carefully transfer to the sheet pan 1 inch (2.5 cm) apart—do not crowd. Paint the turnovers with the egg wash.

4. Bake for 35 minutes, or until golden brown.

5. Remove the sheet pan from the oven and immediately dust the turnovers with the confectioners' sugar, rose petal and pistachio mixture. *Nush-e joon!*

NOTE

Pick over the shelled pistachios carefully to remove any bits of shell that might have remained

SWEET+SAVORY TURNOVERS

sanbuseh

Serves 2 to 4
Prep: 20 minutes
Cooking: 25 minutes

TOMATO SAUCE

2 tablespoons olive oil

4 cloves garlic, peeled and crushed

3 large tomatoes (about 2 lb/900 g), peeled* and chopped, or one 28 oz (800 g) can of Italian plum tomatoes

½ teaspoon ground saffron

½ teaspoon red pepper flakes

2 bay leaves

1 teaspoon sea salt

½ teaspoon freshly ground pepper

PASTA

5 quarts (4.7 liters) water

2 tablespoons sea salt

½ lb (225 g) dried pasta of your choice

1 tablespoon butter or olive oil

GARNISH

½ cup (90 g) freshly grated Parmigiano-Reggiano cheese or goat cheese

1 cup (85 g) shredded fresh Persian basil leaves

SAFFRON, TOMATO, + PERSIAN BASIL PASTA

Recent studies indicate that noodles weren't introduced to Italy from China by Marco Polo in the 13th century. The transfer took place much earlier, in fact, and from the Middle rather than the Far East. Food scholars now believe that pasta is most likely to have originated in Persia, and it was probably the Arabs who introduced noodles, and the hard durum wheat necessary for making it, to Italy in the 9th century. Long before the introduction of the tomato from the new world, ancient Iranians made pasta with a yogurt sauce.

1. To make the sauce: In a large, deep skillet, heat the oil over medium heat. Add the garlic and stir-fry for 30 seconds.

2. Add the tomatoes, saffron, red pepper flakes, bay leaves, salt, and pepper, and sauté for 10 minutes over medium heat. Remove the bay leaves and keep warm until ready to serve.

3. To make the pasta: Just before serving, bring the water to a rolling boil in a large pot.

4. When the water has come to a full boil, add 2 tablespoons salt and the pasta. Stir once and boil for 4 to 12 minutes, depending on the type of pasta (test whether it's done by placing a piece between your teeth).

5. Reserve ¼ cup (60 ml) of the cooking liquid and drain the pasta.

6. Add both the pasta and the reserved liquid to the tomato sauce.

7. Add the butter, toss well, and serve on heated plates. Garnish with grated Parmigiano-Reggiano cheese and fresh basil. *Nush-e joon!*

GREEN SAUCE

Use this sauce to replace the tomato sauce. In a food processor, place 2 cups each of roughly chopped parsley, cilantro, and mint. Add 4 cloves garlic, 1 cup pistachio kernels, juice of 1 lime; ½ cup olive oil, 1 teaspoon salt, ½ teaspoon pepper, and ½ teaspoon red pepper flakes. Purée until you have a smooth paste.

SAFFRON, TOMATO + PERSIAN BASIL PASTA *macaroni*

WALNUT + POMEGRANATE PIZZA

pitza

Makes two 12-inch pizzas
Prep: 20 minutes, plus
  30 minutes for resting
Cooking: 10 minutes per pizza

DOUGH

2 teaspoons active dried yeast

1 cup (240 ml) warm water
  (100°F/40°C)

1 teaspoon granulated sugar

1 tablespoon olive oil

2½ cups (300 g) unbleached
  all-purpose flour, plus
  ½ cup (60 g) for dusting

1 teaspoon sea salt

OLIVE TOPPING

1 cup (8 oz/225 g) pitted
  green olives

2 tablespoons olive oil

1 cup (120 g) shelled walnuts

4 cloves garlic, peeled

1 cup (85 g) chopped fresh
  mint

¼ cup (20 g) chopped fresh
  cilantro

¼ teaspoon dried oregano

½ teaspoon sea salt

¼ teaspoon ground pepper

1 teaspoon red pepper flakes

2 teaspoons ground golpar*
  (optional)

4 teaspoons pomegranate
  molasses*

CHEESE + ONION

Olive oil for brushing and
  drizzling

½ cup (2 oz/50 g) grated
  Parmesan cheese

1 small red onion, peeled and
  sliced

2 cups (175 g) goat-milk
  cheese, crumbled

GARNISH

¼ cup (35 g) pomegranate
  arils (optional)

1 cup (85 g) fresh basil leaves

VE
VEGETARIAN

"Pizza" is the Italian pronunciation for the word pitta, which was how the ancient Greeks used to refer to flat bread from Turkey and Iran. The Italians used the terms pizza as early as the 10th century (though not for a dish with tomatoes, which did not arrive from the New World until much later). The topping combination I have here of olives, walnuts, and pomegranates, popular around the Caspian, goes back at least 3,000 years.

1. To make the dough: In a small bowl, dissolve the yeast in the warm water. Add the sugar and allow to rest, undisturbed, for 5 minutes. Add the oil and stir in.

2. Sift the flour and salt together and place in a food processor, then gradually add the yeast mixture, pulsing between each addition. Mix for 4 minutes, or until you have a sticky dough that comes away easily from the sides of the bowl. Form the dough into a ball and place in a large, oiled bowl. Cover with a damp dish towel and leave to rise for 1 hour at room temperature.

3. Transfer the dough onto a floured work surface, knead for 1 minute and divide into 2 equal pieces. Roll each piece into a ball and place, 6 in (15 cm) apart, on an oiled sheet pan. Cover with plastic wrap and allow to rise, at room temperature, for 20 minutes (or up to 24 hours in the fridge).

4. To make the olive topping: Pulse all the ingredients for the topping in the food processor until you have coarsely chopped mixture.

5. About 20 minutes before serving, preheat the oven to 500°F (260°C) or maximum heat. Heat a 12 in (30 cm) cast-iron skillet on the stovetop over medium-low heat.

6. Brush the skillet with oil, and turn off the heat. Use your hands to shape a dough ball into a 12 in (30 cm) disc. Place the dough flat in the hot skillet (taking care, as the pan is very hot). Brush the dough with oil and scatter with grated Parmesan. Spread half of the olive topping over the dough, then sprinkle over half the onion and goat cheese. Drizzle a little olive oil on top.

7. Place the skillet in the oven (taking care once again, as it's hot and heavy) and bake for 8 to 10 minutes, or until the pizza is golden brown on the edges. Remove from the oven, transfer onto a board and garnish with the pomegranate arils and basil. Cut into slices to share and serve hot before making the next pizza. *Nush-e joon!*

Smoked fish in the Rasht bazaar,
by the Caspian Sea.

FISH

Iran has a surprisingly large variety of fish, and different ways to cook them. The rivers in the foothills of its mountain ranges, such as the Lar River in Damavand, are a fly-fishing paradise. In the north lies the Caspian Sea renowned for its caviar and sturgeon kababs, but also offering a wide range of other delicious white fish. In this region, fish is often simply cooked and flavored with bitter orange, saffron, and sumac (page 130). In the south, the Persian Gulf has some of the least-known yet tastiest varieties of fish and jumbo shrimp in the world. Here, fish is prepared quite differently. One of my favorite recipes involves cooking it in a sauce of cilantro, tamarind, and hot chili peppers, which gives it a uniquely spicy taste (page 132). In fact, this is the only part of Iran where they use chilies in their cooking.

Serves 4
Prep: 20 minutes
Cooking: 20 minutes

FISH WITH VERJUICE + POMEGRANATE

SPICE RUB
2 teaspoons sea salt
½ teaspoon freshly ground
   pepper
1 teaspoon turmeric
1 tablespoon rice flour

FISH
4 thick white fish fillets
   (about 2 lb/900 g),
   or salmon, skin removed

SWEET AND SOUR GLAZE
4 tablespoons pomegranate
   molasses*
1 cup (240 ml) verjuice*
1 teaspoon sea salt
1 tablespoon ground cumin
1 tablespoon ground ginger
1 tablespoon grape molasses
2 tablespoons olive oil

TOPPING
4 cloves garlic, peeled and
   crushed
8 spring onions (white parts
   only)
4 x 4 in (10 cm) cinnamon
   sticks
1 medium tomato, quartered
4 pieces of parchment paper
4 pieces of kitchen thread
   16 inches (40cm) each

GARNISH
½ cup (40 g) basil leaves
½ cup (75 g) pomegranate
   arils

This recipe is from northern Iran, in the Gilan region near the Caspian Sea. Here, I am adding a twist, cooking it in parchment paper (or en papillote as the French call it).

1. Preheat the oven to 450°F (230°C).

2. To make the spice rub: Mix together all the ingredients for the rub in a rimmed sheet pan. Dredge the fish fillets on both sides in the mixture and set aside.

3. To make the glaze: In a sauce pan, combine all the ingredients for the sweet and sour sauce. Bring to a boil, stir well, reduce heat to low and simmer for 2 minutes. Set aside.

4. Spread out a sheet of parchment paper (12 x 16 in/30 x 41 cm) and brush the entire surface with oil. Place 1 fish fillet on the paper in the center, and arrange on top of the fish: 1 clove garlic, 2 spring onions, 1 cinnamon stick, and 1 quarter of the tomato. Pour over 3 tablespoons of the sweet and sour glaze on top.

5. Lift up the edges of the parchment paper and gather them together to enclose the fish in a neat parcel. Use a piece of kitchen thread to tie a tight knot around the top of the parchment paper to stop steam from escaping. Repeat steps 4 and 5 for the remaining fish fillets and place them all on a rimmed sheet pan.

6. Bake in the oven for 20 minutes.

7. Remove from the oven, untie the paper parcels, and pull open to reveal the fish. Garnish with fresh basil and pomegranate arils. Serve the fish, still in the paper, on individual plates, accompanied by a bowl of plain rice (kateh), quinoa, or bulgur for the table. *Nush-e joon!*

FISH WITH VERJUICE + POMEGRANATE

...ba ab ghureh-o anar

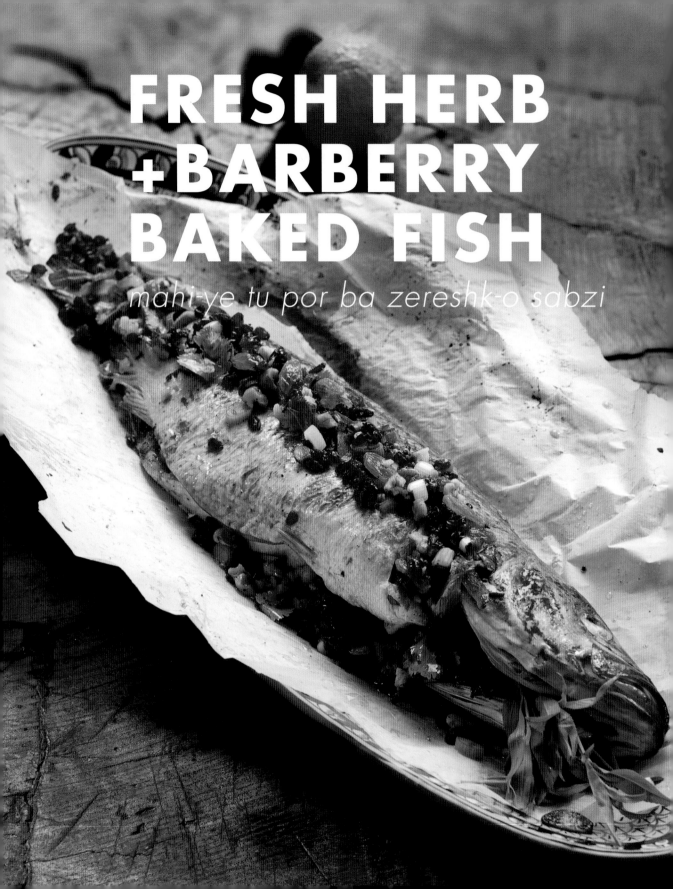

FRESH HERB +BARBERRY BAKED FISH

mahi-ye tu por ba zereshk-o sabzi

Serves 4
Prep: 30 minutes
Cooking: 15 to 20 minutes

TOPPING

¼ cup (60 ml) olive oil

4 cloves garlic, peeled and grated

2 tablespoons chopped fresh tarragon

4 spring onions (white and green parts), chopped

½ cup (40 g) chopped fresh cilantro or parsley

½ cup (40 g) chopped fresh mint

1 cup (85 g) coarsely ground walnuts

½ cup (75 g) dried barberries, cleaned*

½ cup (75 g) seedless raisins

¼ cup (60 ml) fresh lime juice

2 teaspoons sea salt

½ teaspoon freshly ground pepper

FISH

4 fillets of branzino (Mediterranean sea bass), skin on, or 1 large whole fish (see note)

½ cup (120 ml) olive oil

¼ cup (60 ml) fresh lime juice

SPICE RUB

1 teaspoon sea salt

1 teaspoon freshly ground pepper

1 teaspoon turmeric

In the Mazandaran region of the Caspian Sea, where my inspiration for this recipe originated, the locals love to combine lots of fresh herbs with barberries.

1. In a mixing bowl, combine all the ingredients for the topping and toss well together. Set aside.

2. Line a rimmed sheet pan, or baking dish, with a layer of aluminum foil and a layer of parchment paper (allowing extra to overhang the edges of the sheet pan to help lift out the fish). Generously oil the parchment paper.

3. Rinse the fish fillets and pat dry. Lay them side by side on the lined sheet pan, and paint both sides with the olive oil and lime juice.

4. In a small bowl, combine all the ingredients for the spice rub and rub both sides of the fillets with it.

5. Spread a quarter of the topping over each of the fillets. Cover with a layer of oiled parchment paper and keep in the fridge until ready to cook.

6. About 20 minutes before serving, preheat the oven to 400°F (200°C).

7. Bake for 15 to 20 minutes (depending on the thickness of the fillets), or until the fish flakes easily with a fork.

8. Using a large spatula, lift out the fillets and place on individual plates. Baste with the pan juices and serve with rice or quinoa. *Nush-e joon!*

PHOTO NOTE

Photo shows this recipe using a whole fish instead of fish fillets. If you'd like to use a whole fish, have your fishmonger prepare it by cleaning the inside, removing the gills and scales, and scoring the skin. Follow the recipe above, using the topping to stuff the fish and baking, as in steps 6 and 7, for 40 to 45 minutes, or until the fish flakes easily with a fork.

Serves 4
Prep: 10 minutes
Cooking: 8 to 10 minutes

GREEN SAUCE TOPPING

¼ cup (55 g) shelled walnuts

1 cup (85 g) chopped fresh parsley

1 cup (85g) chopped fresh cilantro

1 cup (85 g) chopped fresh mint

4 cloves garlic, peeled and chopped

2 tablespoons lime juice

½ teaspoon sea salt

¼ teaspoon freshly ground pepper

¼ cup (60 ml) olive oil

SUMAC RUB

2 teaspoons sea salt

1 teaspoon freshly ground pepper

1 teaspoon turmeric

¼ cup sumac powder*

FISH

4 fillets of striped bass or catfish (each ½ in/1 cm thick; about 2 lb/900 g total weight)

2 tablespoons olive oil combined with 2 tablespoons lime juice

BAKING OPTION

In step 4, you can bake the fish(instead of grilling) in a preheated 450°F (230°C) oven for 15 to 20 minutes.

The tangy and earthy taste of the sumac contrasts beautifully with lime juice and garlic, and always reminds me of dishes from the Caspian.

1. To make the green sauce topping: In a food processor, pulse all the ingredients for the topping until grainy in consistency (rather than a smooth paste). Keep in the fridge in an airtight, non-reactive container.

2. In a bowl, mix all the ingredients for the sumac rub and set aside.

3. Arrange the fish fillets on a rimmed sheet pan. Brush both sides with the olive oil and the lime juice mixture. Sprinkle the sumac rub all over the fish. Cover with oiled parchment paper, and keep chilled in the fridge until ready to cook.

4. Shortly before you are ready to serve, turn on the broiler and allow it to get good and hot. Remove the cover and place the sheet pan with the fish under the broiler. Broil the fish for 4 to 5 minutes on each side.

5. Take out the sheet pan, place 1 tablespoon of the topping on each fillet, and serve with plain rice (*kateh*). *Nush-e joon!*

GRILLED SALMON MARINATED IN APPLE CIDER VINEGAR + ZATAR

In a quarter-sized rimmed sheet pan (9½ x 13 in/ 24 x 33 cm), place 1 tablespoon sea salt; 1 teaspoon fresh ground pepper; 1 teaspoon ground turmeric; 2 tablespoons zatar (my favorite mix of zatar is sesame, sumac, and thyme); juice and zest of 1 lime; and pour in 1 cup apple cider vinegar. Stir well.

Place a 2-pound (900g) Atlantic salmon fillet (skin-side up) in the sheet pan. Cover and allow to sit for at least 30 minutes, or overnight in the fridge. Preheat broiler until very hot. Cook under the broiler, skin-side down, for 10 minutes, or until done to your liking. Using a spatula, lift up the fish (leaving the skin behind) and serve it without the skin. Squeeze a little lime juice over the fish and garnish with the green sauce above.

SUMAC GRILLED FISH

mahi-e kababi ba somaq

Serves: 4
Prep: 25 minutes
Cooking: 25 minutes

TAMARIND SAUCE

2 tablespoons olive oil

6 cloves garlic, peeled and chopped

½ cup (50 g) chopped spring onions (white and green parts)

3 cups (250 g) chopped fresh cilantro

1 cup (85 g) chopped fresh parsley

1 tablespoon dried fenugreek leaves

2 teaspoons sea salt

½ teaspoon freshly ground pepper

½ teaspoon turmeric

1 teaspoon ground coriander

½ teaspoon red pepper flakes

3 tablespoons rice flour

2 tablespoons tamarind paste dissolved in 2 cups (480 ml) water

2 tablespoons grape molasses*

SPICE RUB

1 tablespoon rice flour

½ teaspoon red pepper flakes

½ teaspoon turmeric

1 teaspoon ground cumin

1 teaspoon ground coriander

¼ teaspoon cinnamon

1 teaspoon sea salt

½ teaspoon freshly ground pepper

FISH

1 lb (450 g) striped bass or catfish fillets, cut into 4 x 3 in (8 cm) pieces

2 tablespoons olive oil

SEARED FISH IN TAMARIND + FENUGREEK SAUCE

This famous dish from the Persian Gulf is one of my all-time favorite ways to cook fish. A young man from Bandar Abbas showed me how his mother made it. The Persian Gulf is known for many things—good and bad, but several varieties of fish and shrimp in that gulf are exceptionally good—Jean Chardin, the jeweler and keen observer also mentions this in the seventeenth century. You can replace the fish with shrimp and follow the recipe exactly as below, except in step 5 sear the shrimp for only a few minutes, shaking the pan back and forth, just until they change color. Take care not to overcook or they will lose their tenderness.

1. Heat the oil in a medium-sized pot over medium heat and sauté the garlic and spring onions for 3 to 5 minutes, or until translucent. Add the cilantro, parsley, and fenugreek, and sauté for 2 minutes longer.

2. Add the salt, pepper, turmeric, ground coriander, red pepper flakes, and rice flour, and sauté for 1 minute.

3. Add the tamarind water and grape molasses, give the mixture a stir, and bring to a boil. Reduce heat to low, cover, and simmer for 20 minutes. Adjust the seasoning to taste and keep warm.

4. In a bowl, mix together all the spice rub ingredients. Dust all sides of the fish and set aside.

5. Just before serving, in a wide skillet, heat the oil over high heat until very hot but not smoking, and sear the fish on each side for 2 to 3 minutes, or until golden brown.

6. Arrange on a serving platter and spoon the tamarind sauce on top.

7. Serve with plain rice (*kateh*) or quinoa. *Nush-e joon!*

SEARED FISH IN TAMARIND + FENUGREEK SAUCE

ghaliyeh mahi

A traditional village
hearth in old Iran.

ROASTS + KABABS

In this section, you'll find a recipe for roast leg of lamb that is infused with pomegranate and cumin. Cooked to perfection, it will just fall off the bone—the way Iranians like their lamb. ☙ Everyone should be able to cook a simple, juicy roast chicken, and I've included a recipe for it here, using a turmeric spice rub to enhance the flavors of the meat. Besides chicken kababs, which are delicious—especially if you use Cornish hens—I couldn't resist giving you an Iranian variation on "fried chicken" that's actually cooked in the oven. ☙ Kababs are delicate pieces of meat and are best eaten hot off the grill; they suffer if kept warm for any length of time after they are done. Make sure everything else is ready before serving the kababs. In my cooking classes everyone is amazed at how easy it is to make the renowned Persian *kubideh* (kababs made from ground meat). If you follow the steps in this book, you will be able to make perfect ground lamb or chicken *kubideh*—and I promise they won't fall off the skewers!

Serves 8 to 10
Prep: 45 minutes
Cooking: 3 hours 45 minutes

POMEGRANATE-INFUSED LEG OF LAMB

1 leg of lamb
   (6 to 7 lb/2.7 to 3.2 kg)
10 cloves garlic, peeled

SPICE RUB
1 teaspoon sea salt
1 teaspoon freshly ground
   pepper
1 teaspoon turmeric
1 tablespoon unbleached all-
   purpose flour

SAUCE
2 medium, yellow onions,
   peeled and quartered
1 cup (120 g) shelled walnuts
3 cups (700 ml)
   pomegranate juice
1 teaspoon sea salt
1 teaspoon red pepper flakes
1 teaspoon freshly ground
   pepper
1 tablespoon ground
   cardamom
1 tablespoon ground cumin

Easy to make, this dish is very tasty and goes particularly well with the Fava and Dill Polow (page 180) or just a green salad. You can prepare the lamb the day before and keep it covered in the fridge until you're ready to bake it. 3 hours and 45 minutes cooking time may seem long, but it's mostly unattended time in the oven. This is a perfect dish for a festive occasion.

1. Preheat the oven to 350°F (180°C).

2. Rinse the leg of lamb and thoroughly pat dry, then place in a non-reactive, large, deep baking dish (preferably one with a lid, such as a cast-iron Le Creuset pot).

3. Use the point of a sharp knife to make 10 slits all over the lamb, then insert the cloves of garlic in the slits. Combine the ingredients for the spice rub and use this to rub all over the lamb.

4. Pulse all the ingredients for the sauce in a food processor until you have a smooth mixture. Spread the sauce over and around the lamb.

5. Cover the baking dish (if you don't have a dish with a lid, use a layer of parchment paper and then a layer of aluminum foil to cover it).

6. Bake the lamb in the oven for 3 hours. Uncover the dish and turn the lamb in its sauce. Continue to bake, uncovered, for 45 minutes, or until the meat is falling off the bone. Transfer it to a serving platter, cover with parchment paper and aluminum foil, and set aside.

7. Place the baking dish on the stovetop and heat the sauce over high heat. Reduce by cooking for 4 to 5 minutes, or until about 1½ cups (350 ml) remain.

8. Serve the lamb with the sauce on the side. *Nush-e joon!*

POMEGRANATE INFUSED LEG OF LAMB

bareh-ye beriyan

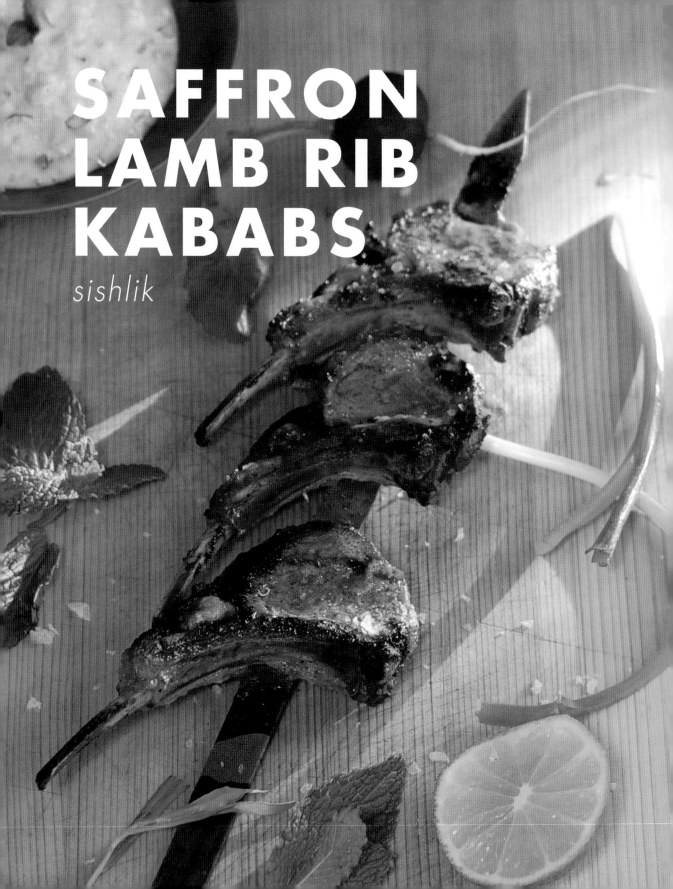

SAFFRON LAMB RIB KABABS

sishlik

Serves 4
Prep: 20 minutes, plus marinating
  for 2 to 3 days
Cooking: 10 minutes

SAFFRON LAMB RIB KABABS

16 small lamb rib chops
  (2 racks, French cut)

MARINADE

1 large onion, peeled and
  thinly sliced

1 bulb garlic (10 to 12 cloves),
  peeled and crushed

Zest of 2 oranges

1 tablespoon honey

1 cup (240 ml) fresh lime
  juice

1 cup (240 g) plain yogurt

2 teaspoons sea salt

1 teaspoon freshly ground
  pepper

½ teaspoon turmeric

2 tablespoons olive oil

½ teaspoon ground saffron
  dissolved in 2 tablespoons
  rose water*

BASTING

2 tablespoons butter

Juice of 2 limes

⅛ teaspoon ground saffron

FOR COOKING + GARNISH

4 thin, flat metal skewers, or
  4 bamboo skewers soaked
  in water for 2 hours

1 x 12 oz (350 g) package of
  lavash bread

½ teaspoon coarse sea salt

Bunch of spring onions

Bunch of fresh basil

1. Place the lamb rib chops in a colander and rinse in cold water. Pat dry thoroughly and place in a large, non-reactive container or bowl.

2. Place all the ingredients for the marinade in a food processor and pulse until you have a grainy sauce. Pour over the lamb and rub each chop thoroughly all over in the marinade. Cover with a lid or plastic wrap and marinate for 2 to 3 days in the fridge. Turn the chops once during this time.

3. Start a bed of charcoal at least 30 minutes before you want to cook, and let it burn until the coals are glowing evenly. If you are using the oven broiler or an indoor grill, make sure it is preheated and very hot.

4. Meanwhile, thread the chops, flat side up, onto the skewers (the skewers will go through the bone, which is soft).

5. For basting, combine the butter, lime juice, and saffron in a small saucepan. Keep warm over very low heat.

6. When the coals are glowing, or the broiler or grill is hot, cook the chops for 4 to 5 minutes on each side, turning occasionally. (The total cooking time should be 8 to 10 minutes.) The chops should be seared on the outside and juicy in the middle. Baste the chops just before removing from the heat.

7. Spread a layer of lavash bread on a serving platter. Place a piece of lavash bread over each skewer and hold it over the chops while you pull out the skewer. Sprinkle with the coarse sea salt. Garnish with the spring onions and basil, cover with lavash bread to keep warm, and serve immediately. *Nush-e joon!*

LIME+TURMERIC ROAST CHICKEN

morgh-e beriyan

Serves 4
Prep: 10 minutes
Cooking: 1½ hours

LIME + TURMERIC ROAST CHICKEN

1 organic or kosher chicken
(3 to 4 lb/1.5 to 1.8 k), or 2
Cornish hens

WET RUB

2 tablespoons olive oil mixed
with ½ cup fresh lime
juice (about 4 limes)

DRY RUB

1 tablespoon sea salt
1 tablespoon freshly ground
pepper
1 tablespoon turmeric
2 tablespoons zatar

STUFFING

1 small onion, peeled and
halved
4 cloves garlic, crushed and
peeled
1 lime, cut in half

BASTE

¼ cup olive oil

1. Preheat the oven to 450°F (230°C). Line a rimmed sheet pan with parchment paper.

2. Place the chicken in a colander and rinse it, inside and outside, with cold water. Pat dry, then place in the lined sheet pan.

3. Pour half of the wet rub mixture inside and half over the chicken, and massage the chicken.

4. In a small bowl, combine all the ingredients for the dry rub, and rub it inside and over the chicken.

5. Stuff the chicken with the onion, garlic, and half a lime.

6. Drizzle some olive oil over the chicken. Cover with another piece of parchment paper and roast for 1½ hours. Remove from oven and baste the chicken

7. Carve and serve, according to your fancy, with any or all of the following: rice, bread, quinoa, salad and/or a fresh herb platter. *Nush-e joon!*

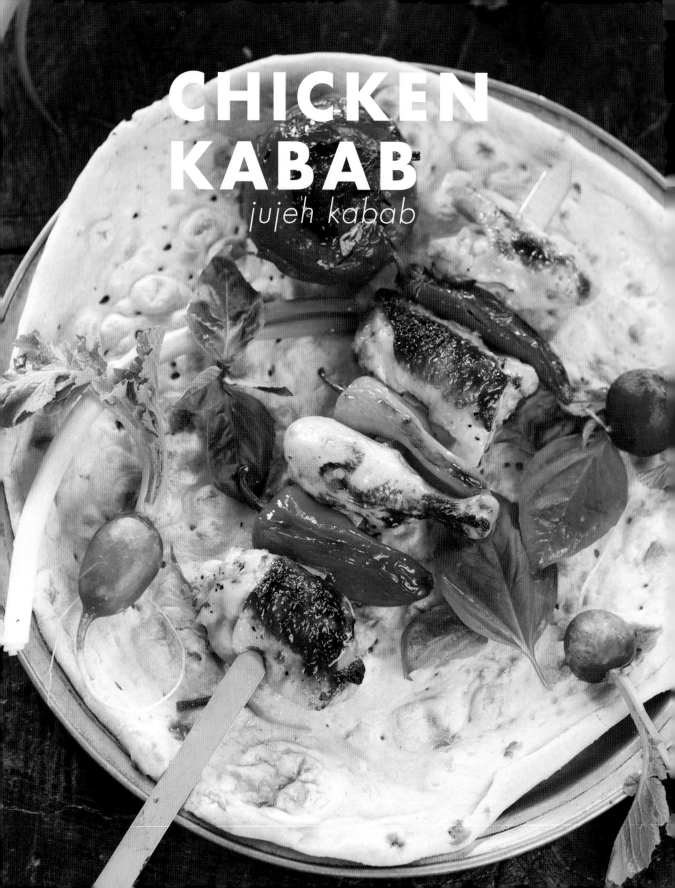

CHICKEN KABAB

jujeh kabab

Serves 4–6
Prep: 20 minutes, plus mari-
  nating for 2 to 3 days
Cooking: 10 to 15 minutes

CHICKEN KABAB

2 Cornish hens
  (about 4 pounds/1.8 k
  total), each cut into 10
  pieces, or 4 pounds of
  chicken drumettes, or 4
  pounds boneless chicken
  thighs cut into 1½–inch
  pieces)

10 cherry tomatoes, or 4
  large tomatoes, quartered

6 jalapeño peppers

MARINADE

2 large onions, peeled and
  quartered

1 clove garlic, peeled

Zest of 2 limes

2 tablespoons fresh lime
  juice

2 tablespoons apple cider
  vinegar

½ cup (120 ml) olive oil

1 cup (240 g) plain yogurt

2 teaspoons sea salt

2 teaspoons freshly ground
  pepper

2 teaspoons turmeric

BASTING

½ cup (110 g) butter

Juice of 1 lime

½ teaspoon sea salt

½ teaspoon freshly ground
  pepper

COOKING & GARNISH

8 flat metal skewers

2 x 12 oz (350 g) packages of
  lavash bread

Lime halves

Fresh parsley sprigs

1. In a colander, rinse the chicken under cold water and pat dry. Place in a large, non-reactive container or bowl.

2. Place all the ingredients for the marinade in a food processor and pulse until you have a grainy sauce. Pour it over the chicken and toss well. Cover with a lid or plastic wrap and leave to marinate in the fridge for at least 2 or up to 3 days. Turn the chicken once during this time.

3. Start a bed of charcoal at least 30 minutes before you want to cook and let it burn until the coals are glowing evenly. If you are using the oven broiler or an indoor grill, make sure it is preheated and very hot.

4. Spear the chicken wings, breasts, and legs on different skewers (they require different cooking times), adding a jalapeño pepper to each skewer. Spear the tomatoes on the separate skewers.

5. For basting, melt the butter in a small saucepan, and add the lime juice, salt, and pepper. Mix well and keep warm over a very low heat.

6. When the coals are glowing, or the broiler or grill is hot, add the kababs, putting the legs on first (if using), then the breasts and wings, drumettes and chicken thighs. Depending on the size of the chicken pieces, grill the kababs for 8 to 15 minutes, turning occasionally. The chicken is done when the juice that runs out is clear rather than pink. Just before removing the kababs from the heat, brush both sides with the basting mixture.

7. Spread a layer of lavash bread on a serving platter and place the kabab skewers on top. Place a piece of bread over each skewer and hold the chicken down while you pull out the skewer. Garnish with halved limes and sprigs of basil and cover with lavash bread to keep warm.

8. Serve immediately with fresh spring onions, basil, and radishes. *Nush-e joon!*

Serves 4
Prep: 20 minutes, plus mari-
  nating for 8 hours to 3 days
Cooking: 30 to 35 minutes

OVEN FRIED CHICKEN

1 broiling chicken (about
  3½ to 4 lb/1.75 to 1.8 k),
  cut into 10 pieces,
  or 4 pounds chicken
  drumsticks, thighs and
  breasts)

MARINADE
2 large onions, peeled and
  quartered
2 cloves garlic, peeled
½ cup (240 ml) apple cider
  vinegar
½ cup (240 ml) olive oil
1 cup (240 g) plain yogurt
2 teaspoons sea salt
2 teaspoons freshly ground
  pepper
1 tablespoon turmeric

COATING
1 cup (150 g) potato
  starch, mixed with 2
  tablespoons poppy seeds
  and 1 tablespoon nigella
  seeds
Coconut oil spray

GARNISH
1 x 12 oz (350 g) package of
  lavash, or any flat bread
2 limes, halved
Sea salt flakes
4 spring onions
1 cup (85 g) fresh basil
  leaves

1. In a colander, rinse the chicken pieces under cold water and pat dry. Place in a large, non-reactive container or bowl.

2. Place all the ingredients for the marinade in a food processor and pulse until you have a grainy sauce. Pour it over the chicken and toss well. Cover with a lid or plastic wrap and marinate in the fridge for at least 8 hours or up to 3 days. Turn the chicken pieces once during this time.

3. Preheat the oven to 450°F (230°C) and line a rimmed sheet pan with parchment paper.

4. Meanwhile, use tongs to remove the chicken pieces from the marinade, shake off any of the marinade ingredients still sticking to the chicken, and place on a plate or sheet pan. Discard the marinade.

5. Tip the potato starch mixture into a resealable plastic bag, add the chicken, and close the bag. Toss the chicken pieces in the potato starch until they are well coated all over.

6. Remove the coated chicken from the bag and spread the pieces out in the lined sheet pan. Spray on top with coconut oil. Bake on the central rack in the oven for 30 to 35 minutes, or until golden brown.

7. When the chicken is done, transfer to a serving platter. Squeeze the lime halves over the chicken and sprinkle with the salt flakes, then garnish with the spring onions and basil. *Nush-e joon!*

STOVETOP FRIED CHICKEN VARIATION

To cook chicken on the stovetop: Fill a large, deep skillet (preferably a cast-iron one) with olive oil to a depth of at least 1 in (2.5 cm) and place over medium-high heat. Heat the oil until it is hot but not smoking (350°F/180°C) and use tongs to gently place the dusted chicken pieces, one by one, into the hot oil. Cover and cook for 4 minutes. Turn the chicken, cover again, and cook for another 4 minutes. Uncover and continue to cook for 2 to 3 minutes, or until cooked through and golden brown all over. Serve as above.

OVEN
FRIED CHICKEN

jujeh-ye sokhari

GROUND CHICKEN KABABS

kabab kubideh-ye jujeh

Serves 6
Prep: 20 minutes, plus chilling
   for 30 minutes to 24 hours
Cooking: 5 minutes

GROUND CHICKEN KABABS

ONION PASTE

1 medium, yellow onion,
   peeled and finely grated
2 cloves garlic, peeled and
   grated
Zest of 1 lime
1 tablespoon olive oil
2 teaspoons sea salt
1 teaspoon fresh ground
   pepper
¼ teaspoon ground saffron
   dissolved in 1 tablespoon
   rose water*

CHICKEN

2 pounds (900 g) ground
   chicken thighs (see note)

BASTING

½ cup (120 ml) olive oil
2 tablespoons fresh lime
   juice

COOKING & GARNISH

12 flat metal skewers
1 x 12 oz (350 g) package of
   lavash bread, or any flat
   bread
2 limes, halved
1 cup (85 g) fresh Persian
   basil leaves*

NOTE

You can use boneless,
skinless chicken thighs to
make your paste. Place in the
food processor with all the
ingredients for the paste (the
onion and garlic quartered
rather than grated). Pulse
until you have a smooth
paste, as in step 2 (do not
over-mix).

1. To make the onion paste: Combine all the ingredients for the paste in a large mixing bowl.

2. Add the ground chicken. Knead with your hands for about 2 minutes. Cover with plastic wrap and chill in the fridge for at least 30 minutes or up to 24 hours.

3. Start the barbecue at least 30 minutes before you want to cook, and let it burn until the coals are glowing evenly. You want the coals to be as high as possible, close to the chicken, and at their hottest. If you are using the oven broiler or an indoor grill, make sure it is preheated and very hot.

4. Using damp hands (keep a bowl of water next to you), divide the chicken paste into 12 equal lumps each about the size of a small orange. Shape each into a 5 in (12.5 cm)-long sausage and mold it firmly around a skewer. Pinch both ends to firmly attach the meat to the skewer. Arrange side by side on an oiled sheet pan. Cover and chill in the fridge until ready.

5. Lay the skewers on the barbecue 3 in (8 cm) above the coals but without touching the grill (bricks on either side make a good platform). *After a few seconds, turn the skewers gently to help meat firm up and to prevent it from falling off. (These first few seconds are important for cooking ground meat kababs.)*

6. Grill the kababs for 5 to 10 minutes, turning frequently. Avoid over-cooking: the meat should be seared on the outside, but juicy and tender in the middle. Baste just before removing from the fire.

7. Place the kabab skewers on the lavash bread platter and cover with the bread to keep warm. When you are ready to serve, place a piece of bread over each skewer and hold the chicken down while you pull out the skewer. Sprinkle with a squeeze of lime and garnish with the fresh basil. Serve with Yogurt & Persian Shallot Dip and Tomato & Cucumber Salad (pages 49 and 66). *Nush-e joon!*

Serves 6
Prep: 20 minutes, plus chilling
  for 30 minutes to 24 hours
Cooking: 5 minutes

ONION MIXTURE

2 medium, yellow onions,
  peeled and finely grated
4 cloves garlic, peeled and
  grated
2 teaspoons sea salt
2 teaspoons freshly ground
  pepper
¼ teaspoon turmeric
2 tablespoons sumac
  powder*
½ teaspoon baking soda
Zest of 1 lime

LAMB

2 lb (900 g) twice-ground
  lamb shoulder, or a
  mixture of 1 lb (450 g)
  each of ground lamb and
  ground beef

BASTING

½ cup (110 g) butter or olive
  oil
1 tablespoon fresh lime juice

COOKING & GARNISH

3 tomatoes, halved
12 flat metal skewers for
  kababs 2 skewers for
  tomatoes
1 x 12 oz (350 g) package of
  lavash bread
½ cup (25 g) sumac powder*
2 limes, halved
1 cup (85 g) fresh Persian
  basil leaves*

1. To make the meat paste: In a large mixing bowl, combine all the ingredients for the onion mixture until grainy.

2. Add the ground lamb and knead with your hands for about 5 minutes. Cover the paste with plastic wrap and chill in the fridge for at least 30 minutes or up to 24 hours.

3. Start the barbecue at least 30 minutes before you want to cook, and let it burn until the coals are glowing evenly. For these kababs, you want the coals to be as high as possible, close to the meat, and at their hottest. Do not spread the charcoal too thinly. If you are using the oven broiler or an indoor grill, make sure it is preheated and very hot.

4. Using damp hands (keep a bowl of water next to you), divide the meat paste into 12 equal lumps each about the size of a small orange. Shape each into a 5 in (12.5 cm)-long sausage and mold it firmly around a skewer. Pinch both ends to firmly attach the meat to the skewer. Arrange side by side on an oiled, rimmed sheet pan. Cover and keep in a cool place.

5. For the baste, melt the butter in a small saucepan and add the lime juice. Keep warm. Spread a layer of lavash bread on a serving platter. Spear the tomatoes on the separate skewers.

6. Lay the skewers on the barbecue 3 in (8 cm) above the coals but without touching the grill (bricks on either side make a good platform). *After a few seconds, turn the skewers gently to help meat firm up and to prevent it from falling off. (These first few seconds are important for cooking ground meat kababs.)*

7. Grill the meat for 3 to 5 minutes, turning frequently. Avoid over-cooking: the meat should be seared on the outside, but juicy and tender in the middle. Baste just before removing from the fire.

8. Place the kabab skewers on the lavash bread platter. Place a piece of bread over each skewer and hold the meat down while you pull out the skewer. Sprinkle with sumac and lime juice to taste. Serve immediately with grilled tomato halves, fresh basil, Yogurt and Persian Shallot Dip (*mast-o musir*, page 49). *Nush-e joon!*

GROUND LAMB KABABS

kabab-e kubideh

Serves 4
Prep: 20 minutes, plus
  marinating for 8 to 24 hours
Cooking: 8 minutes

CASPIAN SWEET + SOUR KABABS

2 lb (900 g) lamb or beef tenderloin or boneless chicken thighs, cut into 2½ in (6 cm) pieces

MARINADE
1 large onion, peeled and quartered
2 cloves garlic, peeled
1 cup (120 g) shelled walnuts
1 tablespoon fresh basil leaves
1 tablespoon fresh mint leaves
2 cups (475 ml) pomegranate juice
2 tablespoons lime juice
¼ cup (60 ml) olive oil
1 teaspoon sea salt
1 teaspoon freshly ground pepper

SWEET + SOUR GLAZE
1 tablespoon pomegranate molasses*
¼ teaspoon freshly ground pepper
½ teaspoon sea salt
¼ teaspoon red pepper flakes (optional)
1 teaspoon ground golpar*
¼ cup (55 g) butter, or (60 ml) olive oil

COOKING + GARNISH
6 flat metal skewers
1 x 12oz (350 g) package of lavash bread
1 cup (150 g) pomegranate arils
1 cup (85 g) fresh basil leaves

Last summer I had the best sweet and sour kabab in a small village near Rasht, by the Caspian Sea. It was served with plenty of herbs and mirza qasemi (Eggplant and Egg Spread, page 100).

1. Place the meat in a non-reactive container or bowl.

2. Combine all the ingredients for the marinade in a food processor and pulse until you have a grainy mixture.

3. Pour over the meat and toss well. Cover with a lid or plastic wrap and marinate in the fridge for at least 8 hours or up to 24 hours.

4. In a saucepan, combine all the ingredients for the glaze and keep warm on very low heat until ready to use.

5. Start the barbecue 30 minutes before you want to cook, and let it burn until the coals glowing evenly. If you are using the oven broiler or an indoor grill, make sure it is preheated and *very hot*.

6. In the meantime, thread 4 or 5 pieces of lamb onto each skewer, leaving at least 2 in (5 cm) free at the top of the skewers. Make sure you skewer the meat against the grain.

7. Once the coals are glowing, place the skewers on the grill and cook for 2 or 4 minutes on each side, turning frequently. When done, baste both sides immediately with the glaze.

8. Spread a layer of lavash bread on a serving platter and place the skewers on the bread. Place a piece of bread over each skewer and hold the meat down while you pull out the skewer. Sprinkle with pomegranate arils and salt. Serve immediately with fresh basil. *Nush-e joon!*

CASPIAN SWEET + SOUR KABABS

kabab-e torsh

Woman attends to her rice field near Rasht by the Caspian Sea.

POLOW + KHORESH

Polow, often called *pilaf* in English, is loosely used by Iranians to refer to any kind of cooked rice. However, technically, *polow* is not just rice but a combination of rice, fruit, herbs, vegetables, and sometimes meat, as reflected in the dishes I've included here. ☙ *Chelow*, for which I've also provided a recipe, is plain rice that has been carefully cooked, parboiled, and steamed. This results in a fluffy rice with each grain well defined, while the bottom of the pot has a crisp, golden-brown crust known as *tah dig.* ☙ *Kateh* is the simplest way of cooking Persian rice, popular around the Caspian, where they eat it even for breakfast. You'll see that I've included a recipe for making it in only 30 minutes. ☙ Khoresh is a braise—a more delicate, refined version of a stew. Ideally khoreshes should be made with fresh, seasonal herbs and vegetables. For a heavy bottomed pot for making khoreshes in this book, I like to use the Le Creuset enameled cast-iron pots, known in America as Dutch ovens, in England as casserole dishes, and in France as *cocottes.* For 4 to 6 people use a 2¾-quart (2.6-liter) pot. These pots are ideal for slow-cooking and keeping the moisture of khoreshes. Natural clay pots—traditionally used in Iran but alo produced by many potters in America today—are excellent too. Khoreshes are usually served on a bed of plain rice—*chelow* or *kateh*. I suggest you serve individual bowls of rice with a little khoresh spooned over each one and garnished with fresh herbs—a traditional style of eating in Iran. In this way, you will experience the taste and aroma of Persian cooking in a single bowl. Everyone will love it, I promise! ℮

In the recipes here, I've reduced the cooking time for many of the khoresh recipes to less than an hour, while retaining the authentic flavor of the original dishes. ℮ Basmati rice from India and Afghanistan makes a good substitute for Iranian rice and has the advantage of being readily available in the U.S. these days. I've used it throughout the recipes in this book. When basmati rice is cooked, it fills the air with a delightful, almost floral aroma. Other kinds of long-grain rice, including the American-grown basmati varieties, may also be used in Persian cooking. ℮ Quinoa is not from Iran, but I cook it in a very similar way to Persian-style rice and often substitute it for rice at home. You could say that adding quinoa to the Persian culinary repertoire merely continues what began with the Silk Road more than two thousand years ago—a mutual exchange between food cultures, each enriching the other in the process.

Chelow Khoresh (or *Polow Khoresh*), a bowl of Saffron Steamed Rice with its golden crust *(tah dig)* with a yogurt braise *(khoresh-e mast)* garnished with toasted almonds, caramelized barberries, and Persian basil.

STOVE-TOP PLAIN RICE

kateh

Serves 4 to 6
Prep: 10 minutes plus 30
  minutes soaking
Cooking: 35 minutes

3 cups (600 g)
   white basmati rice
5½ cups (1.3 liters) water
1 tablespoon sea salt
¼ cup (60 ml) olive oil

STOVE-TOP PLAIN RICE (KATEH)

This is a very simple way to make wonderful rice in only 30 minutes. It is a technique favored around the Caspian, where rice is eaten for breakfast, lunch, and dinner.

1. Wash the rice by placing it in a large container and covering it with water. Agitate gently with your hand, then pour off the water. Repeat 5 times until the water is no longer cloudy. Soak for 30 minutes. Drain, using a fine-mesh colander. If using American long-grain rice, do not wash or soak, and reduce the water to 4½ cups instead of 5½ cups.

2. In a medium-sized pot or saucepan, combine the rice, water, and salt. Gently stir with a wooden spoon to dissolve the salt.

3. Bring to a boil over high heat (this takes about 5 minutes), then reduce heat to medium and simmer, uncovered, for 15 to 20 minutes, or until all the water has been absorbed and the surface of the rice is covered with steam holes.

4. Drizzle the oil over the rice. Cover the pot tightly, the lid wrapped in a clean dish towel, and steam for 15 minutes over low heat. Keep warm until ready to serve.

5. Just before serving, uncover the rice and fluff gently with a fork. *Nush-e joon!*

RICE WITH CILANTRO (DAMI-E GISHNIZ)

In step 4, add 3 cups chopped fresh cilantro with the oil and fluff with two forks.

RICE WITH CUMIN (ZIREH POLOW)

In step 2, add 3 tablespoons black cumin seeds and 1 teaspoon turmeric with the rice, water, and salt. Continue with step 3.

BROWN BASMATI RICE

For brown basmati rice, use 7 cups water instead of 5½ cups and increase the cooking time in step 4 to 30 minutes.

Serves 6
Prep: 10 minutes, plus 30
  minutes soaking
Cooking: 1 hour

RICE-COOKER PLAIN RICE

3 cups (600 g) white basmati
  rice (see headnote)

4 cups (950 ml) water

2 teaspoons sea salt

1 teaspoon ground
  cardamom (optional)

2 tablespoons rose water
  (optional)

½ (120 ml) cup olive oil

SAFFRON

¼ teaspoon ground saffron
  dissolved in 1 tablespoon
  hot water or rose water*

Use a standard measuring cup, not the smaller cup that comes with some rice cookers. The cooking times given here are based on the type of rice cooker available from Iranian markets. If you are using a different brand (such as a Japanese or Chinese rice cooker, not set up for making the golden crust), the timing may be different. You should experiment with yours—allowing between 70 and 90 minutes—to achieve the best results.

1. Wash the rice by placing it in a large container and covering it with water. Agitate gently with your hand, then pour off the water. Repeat 5 times until the water is no longer cloudy. Soak for 30 minutes. Drain, using a fine-mesh colander. If using American long-grain rice, do not wash or soak, and use 3 cups of water instead of 4 cups.

2. In the rice cooker, combine all the ingredients except the saffron water. Gently stir with a wooden spoon for one minute, to help dissolve the salt, cover, and switch on the timer.

3. After 1 hour, drizzle the saffron water over the rice and switch off the rice cooker.

4. Allow to cool for 2 minutes without uncovering the pot.

5. Remove the lid and place a round serving dish (larger than the pot) over the pot. Hold the dish and the pot tightly together and turn them over to unmold the rice. The rice will form a cake with a golden crust (*tah dig*) on top. Cut into wedges and serve. *Nush-e joon!*

BROWN RICE

If using brown basmati rice, you will need 5 cups (1.2 liters) water.

RICE-COOKER PLAIN RICE

kateh ba polow paz

SAFFRON STEAMED RICE

chelow

Serves 6
Prep: 5 minutes
Cooking: 90 minutes

SAFFRON STEAMED RICE (CHELOW)

4 cups (800 g) white
   basmati rice
8 cups (1.9 l) water
2 tablespoons sea salt
2 tablespoons ground
   cardamom (optional)
2 tablespoon rose water
   (optional)

FOR TAH DIG (BOTTOM OF POT)
¾ cup (180 ml) olive oil or
   (110 g) butter
2 tablespoons plain whole
   milk yogurt
½ teaspoon ground saffron
   dissolved in 4 tablespoons
   hot water*

RICE POT

Non-stick pots make
unmolding the rice much
easier. For the ultimate
Persian rice with a good
crust (tah dig), I use a 5-quart
(4.7-liter) pot (11¼ in/28.5 cm
in diameter and 3¼ in/8 cm
deep). The best are hard-
anodized and non-stick,
made by Anolon. They are
available at kitchen equipment stores, Iranian markets,
or via the Internet.

1. Wash the rice by placing it in a large container and covering it with water. Agitate gently with your hand, then pour off the water. Repeat 3 times until the water is no longer cloudy. Drain, using a fine-mesh colander, and set aside.

2. Fill a large, non-stick pot with 8 cups of water, add the salt, cardamom, and rose water, and bring to a boil. Add the rice and boil briskly for 6 to 10 minutes (depending on the type of rice), gently stirring twice with a wooden spoon to loosen any grains that stick to the bottom. Once the rice rises to the top of the pan, it is done.

3. Drain the rice in a large, fine-mesh strainer and rinse with water (about 3 cups/700 ml).

4. In the same pot, combine 2 spatulas of the cooked rice (about 2 cups) with ½ cup oil, the yogurt, ¼ cup water, and 1 tablespoon saffron water. Stir well, using a rubber spatula, until the mixture is smooth and no longer lumpy, then spread out evenly in the pot—this will form the golden crust, or tah dig.

5. Gently heap the remaining rice, 1 spatula at a time, onto the tah dig layer. Shape the rice into a pyramid to allow it to expand.

6. Cover the pot and cook the rice for 10 minutes over medium heat.

7. Mix ½ cup water with ¼ cup oil and pour over the rice. Sprinkle the remaining saffron water on top. Wrap the lid in a clean dish towel to absorb condensation, and place on the pot to prevent any steam from escaping. Reduce heat to low and cook for 70 minutes longer.

8. Remove the pot from the heat and leave it to cool, still covered, on a damp surface (a damp dish towel on a rimmed sheet pan) for 5 minutes to loosen the crust.

9. There are two ways to serve the rice. The first is to hold the serving platter tightly over the uncovered pot and invert the two together, unmolding the entire mound onto the platter. The rice will emerge as a golden-crusted cake, traditionally served in wedges. Or serve the rice straight from the pot and the crust (tah dig) separately.

SAFFRON QUINOA

Quinoa is not from Iran, but South America, where it was first cultivated 3,000 to 4,000 years ago in the Andes. It is not a true cereal, in fact, but more closely related to beetroot and spinach. The Incas considered it a sacred crop and their emperor would traditionally sow the first seeds of the season. Although a very good source of protein, the Spanish colonists dismissed it as "food for Indians." It is much more appreciated today—indeed the United Nations General Assembly declared 2013 as the "International Year of Quinoa." I have included a recipe for it here because it can often be used instead of rice and I cook it in a very similar way. It is a wonderful addition to Persian cooking—especially good if you want to reduce the carbohydrate in your diet—much as the mutual exchange of cooking techniques and ingredients along the Silk Road in years past.

Serves 6
Prep: 5 minutes
Cooking: 30 minutes

3 cups (540 g) quinoa
4 cups (950 ml) water
2 teaspoons sea salt
¼ cup (60 ml) olive oil
¼ teaspoon ground saffron
1 teaspoon ground
   cardamom

1. Wash the quinoa by placing it in a fine-mesh colander and rinsing thoroughly.

2. **To cook the quinoa in a rice cooker:** Place all the ingredients in the rice cooker bowl. Use a long-handled wooden spoon to stir gently for 1 minute to dissolve the salt. Cover, set the rice cooker timer to 30 minutes, and switch on.

   To cook the quinoa on the stovetop: Place all the ingredients in a large pot, stir gently for 1 minute to dissolve the salt, and bring to a boil. Reduce heat to low, cover, and cook for 30 minutes, without stirring.

3. Fluff the cooked quinoa with a fork and serve as you would rice.

_____
VARIATION

Quinoa Barberry Salad

Place 4 cups (640 g) of the cooked quinoa in a salad bowl. Add 1 cup (150 g) caramelized barberries (page 14),* 1 cup (150 g) chopped spring onions, 4 thinly sliced Persian cucumbers (or 1 long seedless cucumber), and 4 thinly sliced radishes. Toss together with ½ cup olive oil, the juice of 1 lime, 2 tablespoons rice vinegar, ½ teaspoon sea salt, and ¼ teaspoon pepper. Adjust the seasoning to taste. *Nush-e joon!*

VEGAN

Serves 6
Prep: 15 minutes; Cooking: 65 minutes

ALMOND + BARBERRY GARNISH
2 tablespoons olive oil

1 cup (6 oz/170 g) whole raw almonds

¼ cup (35 g) seedless raisins

1 tablespoon grape molasses*

1 cup (150 g) dried barberries, cleaned*

CHICKEN
1 onion, peeled and quartered

2 cloves garlic, peeled

1 x 1 in (2.5 cm) fresh ginger root, peeled

¼ teaspoon red pepper flakes

1 celery stalk, cut up

4 tablespoons olive oil

2 teaspoons sea salt

½ teaspoon freshly ground pepper

½ teaspoon turmeric

2 teaspoons ground coriander

2 teaspoons ground cumin

2 teaspoons ground cardamom

½ teaspoon ground cloves

½ teaspoon ground cinnamon

2 bay leaves

2 lb (900 g) skinless, boneless chicken thighs, cut into 4 in (10 cm) pieces

1 tomato, chopped

YOGURT SAUCE
¼ cup (40 g) whole raw almonds

3 tablespoons seedless raisins

1½ cups (360 g) plain yogurt

2 tablespoons fresh lime juice

SALAD TOPPING
1 cup (85 g) fresh basil leaves

4 Persian cucumbers,* peeled and thinly sliced

2 radishes, thinly sliced

YOGURT KHORESH

This wonderful dish is attributed to the chefs of the Mughal court. It's a typically Silk Road dish, incorporating ginger from China, cardamom from India, and yogurt from Iran. In parts of Iran, this khoresh is served with barberries, which is why I have included them in the garnish. It can also be made without meat, tasting equally delicious, simply by replacing the chicken with 1 pound (450 g) of your favorite sliced mushrooms.

1. **To make the almond and barberry garnish:** In a wide skillet, heat 1 tablespoon oil over medium heat until hot. Add the almonds and stir-fry for about 1 minute, or until slightly browned. Add the raisins, give the mixture a stir, transfer to a bowl, and set aside.

   To caramelize the barberries: In the same skillet, place 1 tablespoon oil, 2 tablespoons water, the grape molasses, and the barberries, and stir-fry over medium heat for 4 minutes (be careful, the barberries burn easily). Transfer to another bowl and set aside.

2. **To cook the chicken:** Place the onion, garlic, ginger, chili, and celery in a food processor and pulse until you have a grainy mixture. Set aside.

3. In a medium-sized, heavy-bottomed pot, heat the oil over medium heat until very hot, then add the onion mixture and stir-fry for 2 minutes. Add the salt, pepper, all the spices, bay leaves, and chicken, and sauté for 15 minutes, or until browned. Stir in the tomato, cover, and simmer over low heat for 10 minutes.

4. **To make the yogurt sauce:** In the same food processor, grind the almonds and raisins, add the yogurt, lime juice, and mix for 5 minutes. (This is important as it helps prevent the yogurt from curdling during cooking.)

5. Add the yogurt sauce to the chicken. Cover and simmer over low heat for 45 minutes, stirring occasionally. Remove and discard the bay leaves.

6. Adjust seasoning to taste. Serve the khoresh over plain rice (*kateh*) individually. Garnish with some of the prepared almonds and barberries, and top with some of the basil, cucumbers and radishes. *Nush-e joon!*

YOGURT KHORESH

khoresh-e mast

EGGPLANT KHORESH

khoresh-e bademjan

Serves 4
Prep: 40 minutes
Cooking: 55 minutes

EGGPLANT KHORESH

6 Chinese eggplants (about 3 lb/1.3 kg), peeled and cut in half (see note)

5 tablespoons vegetable oil

3 medium onions, peeled and thinly sliced

2 cloves garlic, peeled and crushed

1 teaspoon sea salt

1 teaspoon freshly ground pepper

½ teaspoon turmeric

½ teaspoon ground cinnamon

1 lb (450 g) skinless, boneless chicken thighs, cut into 2 in (5 cm) strips

½ teaspoon ground saffron dissolved in 4 tablespoons hot water*

3 tomatoes (about 1 lb/450 g), peeled and finely chopped

1 cup (240 ml) water

¼ cup (60 ml) fresh lime juice

1. Preheat the oven to 450°F (230°C).

2. Arrange the eggplants side by side in a oiled sheet pan. Brush each eggplant with a little oil and roast in the oven for 40 minutes. Remove from the oven and set aside.

3. Meanwhile, in a medium-sized, heavy-bottomed pot, heat 3 tablespoons of the oil over medium heat. Add the onions and garlic, and stir-fry for 5 minutes, or until translucent. Add the salt, pepper, turmeric, cinnamon, and chicken and sauté, stirring occasionally, for 10 to 15 minutes longer, or until golden brown.

4. Add the saffron-infused water, tomatoes, water, and lime juice, and bring to a boil. Reduce heat to medium-low, cover, and simmer for 20 minutes.

5. Arrange the eggplants on top of the chicken in the pot. Cover and cook over low heat for 10 to 15 minutes, or until the meat and eggplants are both tender.

6. Adjust the seasoning, adding salt or lime juice, cover again, and keep warm until ready to serve.

7. Serve hot with plain rice (*kateh*) or quinoa. *Nush-e joon!*

NOTE

Chinese eggplants are not bitter, but if you are using Italian eggplants—a deeper purple in color—you will need to salt them first to remove any bitterness. Peel the eggplants, slice in half, and soak in a large container of cold water and 2 tablespoons salt for 20 minutes. Drain, rinse, and thoroughly blot dry.

PHOTO/VARIATION

For the photo on the facing page, I have used 2 pounds (900 g) skinless chicken legs, if you'd like to do the same, increase the cooking time in step 4 from 20 to 40 minutes

APPLE +
CHERRY
KHORESH

khoresh-e sib-o albalu

Serves 4
Prep: 15 minutes
Cooking: 1 hour

APPLE + CHERRY KHORESH

4 tablespoons olive oil

2 medium onions, peeled and thinly sliced

1 teaspoon sea salt

¼ teaspoon freshly ground pepper

½ teaspoon turmeric

½ teaspoon ground cinnamon

1 lb (450 g) skinless, boneless chicken thighs, cut into 2 in (5 cm) pieces

2 cups (475 ml) water

5 firm, tart apples

1 cup (150 g) pitted, dried sour (tart) cherries, or 2 cups (1 lb/450 g) fresh pitted cherries

2 tablespoons grape molasses*

3 tablespoons apple cider vinegar

½ teaspoon ground saffron dissolved in 2 tablespoons hot water* (optional)

Using fruit and nuts to create a slow-cooked braise with a sweet and sour flavor has been part of Persian cooking since ancient times (we have references to it as far back as the 6th century). This is a wonderfully easy recipe to make and delicious. I use Fuji apples, but you can use any kind of firm apple, and dried tart cherries are readily available everywhere in the U.S. these days.

1. In a medium-sized, heavy-bottomed pot, heat 2 tablespoons oil over medium heat and sauté the onions for 5 minutes, or until translucent. Add the salt, pepper, turmeric, and cinnamon, and give everything a stir. Add the chicken and sauté for 10 to 15 minutes, or until brown.

2. Add the water and bring to a boil. Reduce heat to medium-low, cover and simmer for 10 minutes, stirring occasionally.

3. Meanwhile, core the apples and cut them into wedges. In a large skillet, heat 2 tablespoons oil over medium-high heat and sauté the apples for 10 to 15 minutes, shaking the skillet back and forth, until golden brown all over. Add the cherries, grape molasses, vinegar, and saffron, and stir gently for 1 minute. Remove from heat.

4. Add the apple and cherry mixture to the chicken and gently stir together. Cover and cook over medium-low heat for 10 to 15 minutes, or until the apples and chicken are tender.

5. Taste the khoresh—it should taste sweet and sour. Adjust the seasoning, adding grape molasses or vinegar if necessary. Cover and keep warm until ready to serve.

6. Serve hot with rice or quinoa, and a platter of fresh herbs on the side. *Nush-e joon!*

VEGETARIAN VARIATION

For a vegetarian version, replace the chicken with ½ cup (100 g) split peas (or mung beans), and sauté for only 1 minute. Add these in step 2 with 4 cups (950 ml) water (instead of just 2 cups). Proceed with the recipe as above.

VEO
VEGETARIAN
OPTION

Serves: 4
Prep: 30 minutes, plus soaking
   the beans overnight
Cooking: 1 hour

1½ cups (300 g) dried
   red kidney beans,
   soaked overnight with
   ½ teaspoon baking soda,
   drained and rinsed*
1 leek, cut up (white and
   green parts)
1 medium onion, peeled and
   quartered
4 cloves garlic, peeled
4 cups (225 g) fresh baby
   spinach
2 cups (175 g) fresh parsley,
   roughly cut up or 2/3 cup
   dried
2 cups (175 g) fresh cilantro,
   roughly cut up or 2/3 cup
   dried
4 tablespoons olive oil
2 tablespoons dried
   fenugreek leaves
   (see note)
1 tablespoon sea salt
1 teaspoon freshly ground
   pepper
1 teaspoon turmeric
4 whole dried Persian limes,*
   pierced in several places
   with the point of a knife
4 cups (950 ml) water
1 teaspoon grape molasses*
½ cup (120 ml) fresh lime
   juice (about 4 limes)

NOTE
Dried fenugreek leaves,
available at Iranian markets,
are essential for the taste of
this dish. Do not substitute
with fenugreek seeds.

FRESH HERB KHORESH

This is probably one of every Iranian's favorite khoreshes. My mother would spend all day preparing the dish, chopping all the herbs, and cooking it. Here, however, I've made it meatless, and given a few shortcuts, so it can be cooked in an hour, while tasting just as delicious.

1. Place the leek, onion, and garlic in a food processor and pulse until finely chopped. Remove and set aside.

2. Place the spinach, parsley, and cilantro in the food processor and pulse until the herbs are finely chopped (but not puréed). Set aside.

3. In a medium-sized, heavy-bottomed pot, heat the oil over medium heat. Add the leek, onion, and garlic mixture and sauté for 5 minutes.

4. Add the chopped herbs and fenugreek, and fry for 10 minutes, stirring *frequently*, until the aroma of the herbs rises. (This stage is very important: the herbs should be cooked enough to ensure the braise has the right flavor, but take care to not burn them.) Add the salt, pepper, turmeric, and Persian limes and the beans, and stir-fry for 1 minute.

5. Add the water and grape molasses to the pot, and bring to a boil. Give it a stir, then reduce heat to medium-low, cover, and simmer for 40 to 45 minutes, or until the beans are tender, stirring occasionally.

6. Add the lime juice and adjust the seasoning to taste. Cover and keep warm until ready to serve.

7. Serve hot with plain rice (*kateh*). *Nush-e joon!*

FRESH HERB KHORESH

khoresh-e ghormeh sabzi

CELERY + MUSHROOM KHORESH

½ cup (120 ml) olive oil

1½ pounds (675 g) crimini mushrooms, cleaned and thickly sliced

1 bunch (8 stalks) celery, washed and julienned (¼-inch/6 mm)

1 medium onion, peeled and thinly sliced

2 cloves garlic, peeled and thinly sliced

1 jalapeno pepper, thinly chopped or ½ teaspoon red pepper flakes

2 teaspoons sea salt

½ teaspoon freshly ground pepper

½ teaspoon turmeric

3 tablespoons dried fenugreek leaves

2 teaspoons grape molasses

3 cups (930 ml) water

½ teaspoon ground saffron dissolved in 2 tablespoons water* (optional)

3 tablespoons fresh lime juice

1 cup (80 g) chopped fresh parsley or 1/3 cup dried

½ cup (40 g) chopped fresh mint, or 3 tablespoons dried

This khoresh (braise) is traditionally made with lamb, which I have replaced here with crimini mushrooms to create a perfect vegan khoresh. Crimini mushrooms have an earthy taste and keep their shape when cooked, but you can use any other kind of mushroom. Try this simple recipe over rice (kateh) or quinoa, and you will find that it keeps the authentic flavors of the very popular Persian celery khoresh.

1. Heat the oil in a medium-sized, heavy-bottomed pot over high heat. Add the mushrooms and sauté for 5 to 10 minutes until all juices have been absorbed. Add the celery, onion, garlic, and jalapeno pepper, and sauté for 10 minutes. Add the salt, pepper turmeric, fenugreek, and grape molasses, and give it a stir.

2. Add the water and bring to a boil. Reduce heat to medium, cover, and simmer for 40 minutes.

3. Add the saffron, lime juice, parsley, and mint, and give it a stir. Reduce heat to medium-low, cover, and simmer for another 5 minutes or until the celery is tender.

4. Adjust seasoning to taste and keep warm until ready to serve. *Nush-e joon!*

CROCK-POT OR SLOW COOKER METHOD FOR MAKING KHORESHES

Slow cookers, with their ceramic pots and even cooking temperatures over long unattended periods, are excellent for cooking khoreshes. The trick is to first heat the oil in a large, wide skillet and caramelize the onion. Then transfer the onion and the rest of the ingredients for the khoresh to the pot. Cover, set temperature to high and the time to 4 hours (or you can set the temperature to low and the time to 8 hours).

CELERY + MUSHROOM KHORESH

Khoresh-e karafs

POTATO + SPLIT PEA KHORESH

khoresh-e qeymeh

Serves 4
Prep: 20 minutes
Cooking: 1 hour

POTATO + SPLIT PEA KHORESH

POTATO

2 Russet potatoes
(1½ lb/670 g), peeled,
julienned, and soaked
in cold water for at least
15 minutes, drained, rinsed
and thoroughly dried

1 tablespoon olive oil

½ teaspoon sea salt

KHORESH

4 tablespoons olive oil

2 large onions, peeled and
thinly sliced

2 teaspoons sea salt

1 teaspoon freshly ground
pepper

½ teaspoon turmeric

1 lb (450 g) boneless, skinless
chicken thighs, cut into 1 in
(2½ cm) cubes

4 whole dried Persian limes,*
pierced in several places
with the point of a knife

¼ cup (50 g) yellow split
peas

2 cups (450 g) fresh or
canned tomatoes, peeled*
and chopped

2 cups (470 ml) water

1 teaspoon ground cinnamon

Zest of 2 oranges

1 teaspoon ground saffron
dissolved in 3 tablespoons
orange blossom water*

¼ cup fresh lime juice

1 teaspoon honey

I have made this khoresh with oven baked fries to reduce the amount of oil used. For a vegetarian version, eliminate the chicken from step 3 and increase the split peas in step 4 to ½ cup and the water to 4 cups. Everything else remains the same.

1. Preheat oven to 350°F (180°C). Line a baking sheet with parchment paper. Place the potato strips in a resealable plastic bag with 1 tablespoon oil and ½ teaspoon salt, seal and shake the bag to evenly coat the potatoes. Tip the coated potatoes into the sheet pan and spread in an even layer.

2. Bake in the oven for 45 to 50 minutes. Remove from the oven, sprinkle with a little salt and set aside.

3. Meanwhile, in a medium-sized, heavy-bottomed pot, heat 4 tablespoons oil over medium heat. Add the onions and sauté until translucent. Add the salt, pepper, and turmeric, and stir-fry 1 minute. Add the chicken and the dried Persian limes, and sauté for 15 to 20 minutes longer, stirring occasionally, until the chicken is golden brown and all the juices have been absorbed.

4. Add the split peas and sauté for 1 minute.

5. Add the tomato, 2 cups water, cinnamon, orange zest, saffron orange blossom water, lime juice, and honey, and bring to a boil. Reduce heat to medium-low, cover and simmer for 30 to 45 minutes (depending on type of yellow split peas), until the split peas are tender (do not over cook; split peas should not be mushy).

6. Adjust seasoning to taste by adding more salt or lime juice. Cover, and keep warm until ready to serve.

7. Just before serving, arrange the potatoes on top of the khoresh. Serve hot with rice and a fresh herb platter. *Nush-e joon!*

Serves 4 to 6
Prep: 25 minutes
Cooking: 30 minutes

½ cup (120 ml) olive oil or (110 g) butter

7 cloves garlic, peeled and thinly sliced

3 lb (1.3 kg) fresh fava beans in the pod, or 1 lb (450 g) frozen fava (second skins removed), you can also use, lima beans or edamame

1½ teaspoons fine sea salt

½ teaspoon pepper

1½ teaspoons turmeric

1½ cups (120 g) chopped fresh dill weed, or ½ cup (40 g) dried

1 tablespoon rice flour dissolved in 2 cups (480 ml) water

4 large eggs, chicken or duck

NOTES

Frozen fava beans with second skins already removed are available at Iranian markets.

You can replace fava beans with 1 can cooked whole beans, drained and rinsed. Everything else remains the same

Around the Caspian they refer to khoresh as qataq. This khoresh is a perfect vegetarian dish when served over rice. Locals make this dish using a type of fava bean called pachlaq, *which is long and white. But it's also delicious made with fresh fava beans, lima beans, or even edamame. The photo shows the khoresh slow cooked in a clay pot (gamaj), which I bought in the Rasht bazaar by the Caspian Sea. On the table, the pot sits on its own wicker base (gamaj daneh).*

1. If using fresh fava beans in the pod, shell and skin them. For frozen ones allow them to thaw for 5 minutes. Drain and rinse in a colander. Set aside.

2. In a medium-sized, heavy-bottomed pot, heat the oil over medium-low heat. Add the garlic and sauté for 2 minutes. Add the beans, salt, pepper, and turmeric, and sauté for 1 minute. Add the dill and sauté for 2 minutes

3. Add the rice flour-water, and bring to a boil. Reduce heat to low, cover, and cook for 5 to 10 minutes, or until the beans are tender.

4. Just before serving, make 4 holes in the beans, drop 1 egg in each hole, and sprinkle with salt and pepper. Simmer over low heat for 10 to 15 minutes, until the eggs are set. Give the mixture a stir and adjust the seasoning to taste.

5. Serve immediately over plain rice (*kateh*), quinoa, bread or tortillas, with thick yogurt. *Nush-e joon!*

CASPIAN FAVA + EGG KHORESH

bagala qataq

Serves: 4
Prep: 30 minutes
Cooking: 1 hour

FOR BUTTERNUT SQUASH
1 large butternut squash
(about 3 lb/1.35 kg), peeled
and cut into ½-inch
(1.75 cm) cubes*
½ teaspoon sea salt
½ teaspoon ground pepper
1 tablespoon olive oil

FOR WALNUT SAUCE
2 tablespoons olive oil
2 medium onions, peeled
and sliced
1 teaspoon sea salt
½ teaspoon ground pepper
½ teaspoon turmeric
½ teaspoon ground
cinnamon
1 tablespoon ground
cardamom
2 teaspoons ground cumin
3 cups (about 13 oz/360 g)
shelled walnuts
2 cups (120 g) chopped fresh
parsley
2 cups (120 g) chopped fresh
cilantro
2 cups (120 g) chopped fresh
mint
Zest of 1 orange
4 cups (950 ml) fresh
pomegranate juice
1 teaspoon pomegranate
molasses*
1 teaspoon grape molasses*

GARNISH
1 cup (150 g) pomegranate
arils (1 pomegranate)
Sprigs of cilantro

Traditionally this recipe is made with duck: the affinity between pomegranate and duck in Persian cooking goes back to ancient times. However, this dish is equally delicious—and nutritious—made without meat, which is what I am giving you here. For those who'd like meat, I suggest serving it with chicken kabab (page 143).

1. ***To roast the butternut squash:*** Preheat oven to 400°F (200°C). Line a rimmed sheet pan with parchment paper. Place the butternut squash cubes with the salt, pepper, and olive oil in the pan, toss well and spread evenly. Roast in the preheated oven for 15 minutes, until tender. Set aside.

2. ***To make the walnut sauce:*** In a medium-sized, heavy-bottomed pot, heat 2 tablespoons oil over medium heat. Add the onions and sauté for 10 to 15 minutes, until golden brown. Add the salt, pepper, turmeric, cinnamon, cardamom, cumin, and walnuts, and sauté for 1 minute.

3. Transfer the onion and walnut mixture to the food processor. Add the parsley, cilantro, and mint and finely grind. Add 1 cup (only) of the pomegranate juice, the orange zest, pomegranate molasses, and grape molasses, and mix well to create a smooth, creamy sauce.

4. Return the sauce to the pot, add the remaining pomegranate juice (3 cups), half of the roasted butternut squash (keep the other half for garnish), and bring to a boil. Reduce heat to *low*, cover, and simmer for 45 minutes, stirring occasionally with a wooden spoon to prevent the walnut from burning.

5. Taste the khoresh and adjust the seasoning. This khoresh should be sweet and sour: If too sweet, add extra pomegranate molasses; if too sour, add a little more grape molasses

6. Cover and keep warm until ready to serve. Just before serving, garnish with the remaining butternut squash, pomegranate arils, and sprigs of cilantro. Serve hot with rice or quinoa. *Nush-e joon!*

POMEGRANATE + WALNUT KHORESH

khoresh-e fesenjan

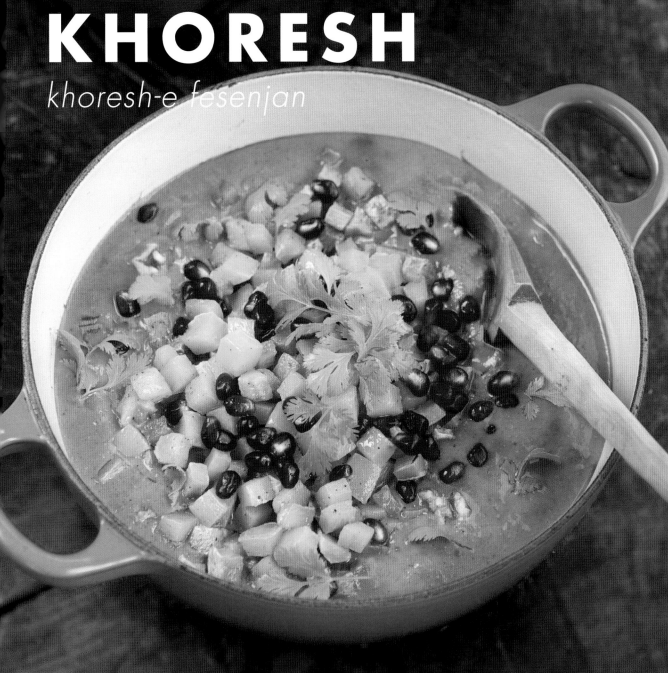

Servings: 6
Prep: 45 minutes
Cooking: 30 minutes

2 cups (400 g) white basmati rice

3 lb (1.3 kg) fresh fava beans, or 1 lb (450 g) frozen, second skins removed

½ cup (120 ml) olive oil

1 x 4 in (10 cm) cinnamon stick

1 leek (white and green parts), finely chopped

4 cloves garlic, peeled and grated

2 teaspoons sea salt

½ teaspoon freshly ground pepper

¼ teaspoon turmeric

2 tablespoons ground cardamom

2 tablespoons rose water

3 cups (700 ml) water

3 cups (250 g) coarsely chopped fresh dill weed, or 1 cup dried

½ teaspoon ground saffron dissolved in 2 tablespoons rose water*

1. Wash the rice by placing it in a large container and covering it with water. Agitate gently with your hand, then pour off the water. Repeat 5 times until the water is no longer cloudy. Soak for 30 minutes. Drain, using a fine-mesh colander, and set aside.

2. If using fresh fava beans in the pod, shell and skin them. If using frozen fava beans, allow to thaw. Drain, rinse and set aside.

3. Heat ¼ cup oil in a large, non-stick pot until very hot. Add the cinnamon stick, leek, and garlic, and stir-fry for 5 minutes, or until the leek is wilted. Add the rice, salt, pepper, turmeric, cardamom, and rose water, and stir-fry for another 1 minute.

4. Add the water, tip in the skinned fava beans and bring back to a boil, stirring gently twice with a wooden spoon. Cover firmly with a lid to prevent any steam from escaping. *Reduce heat to medium* and cook for 12 to 15 minutes, or until all the water has been absorbed.

5. Add the dill and fluff using 2 forks. Drizzle the remaining oil and the saffron-infused rose water over the rice. Cover again, *reduce heat to low,* and cook for another 10 minutes. Remove the pot from heat and allow to cool, still covered, for 5 minutes.

6. Transfer to a serving dish and serve with fried eggs, yogurt and Persian shallots (page 49), or roasted lamb (page 136) or fish (page 130). *Nush-e joon!*

_____

VARIATION

You can replace the fava beans with shelled lima or edamame beans, fresh or frozen. You can also replace the rice with 2 cups (360 g) quinoa (thoroughly rinsed). Everything else remains the same.

FAVA + DILL POLOW

baqala polow

CARAMELIZED BARBERRY + CARROT POLOW

javaher polow

Serves 6
Prep: 40 minutes
Cooking: 25 minutes

CARAMELIZED BARBERRY + CARROT POLOW

2 cups (400 g) white basmati
  rice

½ (120 ml) cup olive oil

3 large carrots (about 225 g),
  peeled and julienned

Zest of 3 oranges

1 cup (200 g) sugar

1 tablespoon orange blossom
  water*

1 teaspoon ground
  cardamom

½ teaspoon ground
  cinnamon

3 cups (700 ml) water

1 cup (150 g) dried barberries,
  cleaned*

2 tablespoons slivered
  almonds

2 tablespoons slivered
  pistachio kernels

Served with a fresh herb platter and/or a green salad, this wonderfully tasty vegetarian dish makes a meal in itself, but it works equally well as an accompaniment to roast chicken or lamb. You can substitute the barberries with 1½ cups (225 g) semi-sweet dried cranberries. There is no need to caramelize these—just add them in step 5 with the almonds and pistachios.

1. Wash the rice by placing it in a large container and covering it with water. Agitate gently with your hand, then pour off the water. Repeat 3 times until the water is no longer cloudy. Soak the rice for 30 minutes. Drain, using a fine-mesh colander, and set aside.

2. In a large, non-stick pot, heat ¼ cup oil over medium heat and sauté the carrots and orange zest for 1 minute. Add ¾ cup of the sugar, along with the orange blossom water, cardamom, and cinnamon. Tip in the rice and stir-fry for 2 minutes.

3. Add the water and give the pot a gentle stir. Cover and cook over medium heat for 12 to 15 minutes, or until all the water has been absorbed.

4. To caramelize the barberries: In a wide skillet, combine 2 tablespoons water, 2 tablespoons of the oil, 2 tablespoons of the sugar, and the barberries, and stir-fry for 4 minutes over medium heat (taking great care as barberries burn easily). Remove the pan from heat and set aside.

5. Add the caramelized barberries to the rice with the almonds and pistachios. Drizzle the remaining oil over the rice and fluff gently with a fork. Cover tightly and cook for 10 minutes over medium-low heat.

6. Remove from heat and allow to sit, still covered, for 5 minutes.

7. Remove the lid and gently transfer the rice onto a serving platter. *Nush-e joon!*

LENTIL+DATE POLOW

adas polow

Serves 6
Prep: 10 minutes
Cooking: 45 minutes

LENTIL + DATE POLOW

2 cups (400 g) white basmati rice

1 cup (200 g) green lentils, rinsed

6 cups (1.5 l) water

1 cup (150 g) seedless raisins

1 cup (175 g) pitted dates, chopped

½ (120 ml) cup olive oil

4 medium onions, peeled and thinly sliced

2 teaspoons sea salt

½ teaspoon freshly ground pepper

1 x 4 in (10 cm) cinnamon stick

2 teaspoons ground cardamom

2 tablespoons granulated sugar

Zest of 2 large oranges

1. Wash the rice by placing it in a large container and covering it with water. Agitate gently with your hand, then pour off the water. Repeat 3 times until the water is no longer cloudy. Soak for 30 minutes. Drain, using a fine-mesh colander, and set aside.

2. Place the lentils and 3 cups of the water in a large saucepan and bring to a boil. Reduce the heat to medium and cook for 15 to 20 minutes, or until the lentils are tender. Drain the lentils (do not rinse), add the raisins and dates, toss well, and set aside.

3. Meanwhile, in a large, non-stick pot, heat ¼ cup oil over medium heat. Add the onions and sauté for 10 to 15 minutes, until golden brown. Add the rice, salt, pepper, cinnamon stick, cardamom, sugar, and orange zest, and stir-fry for 1 minute.

4. Add 3 cups of water, give the pot a gentle stir, cover, and cook over medium heat for 12 to 15 minutes, or until all the water has been absorbed.

5. Add the lentil mixture to the rice and drizzle the remaining oil over the top. Fluff gently with a fork, then cover and cook over low heat for 10 minutes. Keep the rice warm until ready to serve.

6. Serve with your favorite green salad, fresh herbs, and pickles. *Nush-e joon!*

VARIATION

Replace the rice with 2 cups (360 g) quinoa and follow the recipe in the same way. While quinoa, unlike basmati rice, doesn't need to be washed, it should be rinsed thoroughly in a fine-mesh colander before using.

Serves 6
Prep: 30 minutes plus 30
  minutes soaking
Cooking: 55 minutes

2 cups (400 g) white basmati
  rice
½ (120 ml) cup olive oil
2 medium onions, peeled
  and thinly sliced
4 cloves garlic, peeled and
  sliced
1 tablespoon sea salt
1 teaspoon freshly ground
  pepper
½ teaspoon turmeric
½ teaspoon cayenne
1 x 4in (10 cm) cinnamon
  stick
1½ lb (680 g) fresh green
  beans, cut into 1 in (2.5 cm)
  lengths, or 10 oz (275 g)
  ready-cut frozen green
  beans
3 large tomatoes (about
  1 lb/450 g), peeled*
  and diced, or 3 cups
  (1½ lb/675 g) canned
  tomatoes, drained
2 tablespoons fresh lime
  juice

Rice with green beans and tomatoes tends to be everyone's favorite dish, children included. With everything cooked in one pot, this is a quick and easy way to make it. For a non-vegan version, simply add 1 pound ground lamb, chicken, or turkey, sautéed with the onions in step 2.

1. Wash the rice by placing it in a large container and covering it with water. Agitate gently with your hand, then pour off the water. Repeat 3 times until the water is no longer cloudy. Soak for 30 minutes. Drain, using a fine-mesh colander, and set aside.

2. Heat ¼ cup oil in a large, non-stick pot over medium heat until very hot. Add the onions and garlic, and sauté for 15 minutes until golden brown. Add the salt, pepper, turmeric, cayenne, and cinnamon stick. Tip in the green beans and stir-fry for 1 minute. Add the rice and stir-fry for another minute.

3. Add the tomatoes and lime juice, and stir gently with a wooden spoon. Cover the pot firmly and cook over medium heat for 8 to 10 minutes, or until all the liquid has been absorbed.

4. Drizzle the remaining oil and 1 cup water over the rice. Cover tightly and allow to cook over a low heat for another 30 minutes. Keep warm until ready to serve.

5. Remove the pot from the heat and allow to cool, still covered, on a damp surface (a damp dish towel on a rimmed sheet pan) for 5 minutes to loosen any crust. Transfer to a serving dish and serve with Tomato & Cucumber Salad (page 66) and fresh basil. *Nush-e joon!*

GREEN BEAN + TOMATO POLOW

lubia polow

SOUR CHERRY POLOW

albalu polow

Servings: 6
Prep: 30 minutes
Cooking: 40 minutes

2 cups (400 g) white basmati rice

½ (120 ml) cup olive oil

2 medium onions, peeled and thinly sliced

1 x 4 in (10 cm) cinnamon stick

2 teaspoons sea salt

½ teaspoon freshly ground pepper

1 teaspoon ground cardamom

2½ cups (375 g) pitted, dried tart/sour cherries (see note)

3 cups (700 ml) water

½ teaspoon ground saffron dissolved in 2 tablespoons hot water* (optional)

1 cup (240 ml) sour cherry syrup (see note below)

½ cup (60 g) slivered almonds

½ cup (60 g) slivered pistachio kernels

NOTE

You can replace the dried cherries and the syrup with 3 cups pitted sour cherries, fresh or frozen, cooked with ½ cup (100 g) granulated sugar for 15 minutes over high heat. Bottled ready-made sour cherry syrup is available in Iranian markets.

Tart or sour cherries have become increasingly common in the U.S. The fresh cherries can be bought in July at local Iranian markets, while the dried ones are available throughout the year in most supermarkets. Quick and easy to prepare, this recipe makes a delicious vegetarian dish, but it's also wonderful with roast chicken, a traditional dish in Iran (albalu polow ba jujeh), or chicken kababs.

1. Wash the rice by placing it in a large container and covering it with water. Agitate gently with your hand, then pour off the water. Repeat 3 times until the water is no longer cloudy. Drain, using a fine-mesh colander, and set aside.

2. Heat ¼ cup oil in a large, non-stick pot over medium heat and add the onions. Sauté for 10 to 15 minutes, stirring occasionally, until golden brown.

3. Add the cinnamon stick, salt, pepper, cardamom, rice, and cherries, and stir-fry for 1 minute. Add the water and give it a stir with a wooden spoon, then cover and cook over medium heat for 12 to 15 minutes, or until all the water has been absorbed.

4. Add the saffron water, sour cherry syrup, almonds, and pistachios, and fluff gently with a fork. Reduce heat to low, cover firmly, and cook for 10 minutes longer. Remove the pot from heat and allow to sit, still covered, for 5 minutes

5. Transfer to a serving dish and present alongside roast chicken and a fresh herb platter, as it is traditionally served in Iran. I find that a green salad also works well with this dish.

Serves 6
Prep: 20 minutes
Cooking: 1 hour

½ cup (120 ml) olive oil

2 large onions, peeled and thinly sliced

2 cloves garlic, peeled and chopped

2 serrano chilies, chopped, or 1 teaspoon red pepper flakes

1-inch fresh ginger, peeled and grated

1 cup (180 g) coarse bulgur

1 tablespoon sea salt

½ teaspoon freshly ground pepper

1 teaspoon turmeric

2 tablespoons ground cumin

2 tablespoons tomato paste

1 cup (200 g) dried mung beans, rinsed

2 medium tomatoes, peeled* and diced (2 cups)

4½ cups (1 l) water

4 cups (340 g) chopped fresh dill weed (stems included)

Bulgur is made by removing the husks from wheat, then steaming, drying and crushing the berries. It's an ancient way of preparing wheat and used to be a popular ingredient in Persian cooking, but around the fifteenth century rice began to take its place. Dami is the Persian term for grains mixed with herbs and cooked in one pot. The combination of bulgur, with dill and mung beans results in a perfectly balanced dish, especially nutritious for vegetarians and vegans.

1. In a large, non-stick pot, heat ¼ cup oil over medium heat until very hot. Add the onions and garlic, and sauté for 10 minutes, or until golden brown. Add the chilies, ginger, bulgur, salt, pepper, turmeric, cumin, and tomato paste, and stir-fry for 1 minute.

2. Add the mung beans, diced tomato, and the water. Stir gently once and bring to a boil. Reduce heat to medium, cover, and cook for 40 to 50 minutes, or until the beans and bulgur are tender, and the water has been absorbed completely.

3. Add the dill, and drizzle the remaining oil on top. Fluff gently with a fork, then cover and keep warm until ready to serve.

4. Serve on the side with fried eggs or roast chicken or lamb, or on its own with a salad. *Nush-e joon!*

BULGUR + MUNG BEAN DAMI WITH DILL

dami-e balghur-o mash

Clockwise from top left: **Fig-peaches, pomegranate arils (seeds), fresh dates, figs, pistachio kernels.**

DESSERTS + TEAS

The word "dessert," referring to a sweet dish usually eaten at the end of a meal, was first used in France in the sixteenth century. However, the tradition of eating a sweet course at the end of the meal goes back over 2,500 years to the ancient Persians. As far back as the fifth century BCE, Herodotus, the "father of history," wrote: "The Persians believe that the Greeks finish their dinner still hungry because they don't have any worthwhile desserts." Iranians believed that finishing with sweets helped digest the meal. ✑ At the end of a meal Iranians would clear away the sofreh (everything laid out on the table) and prepare a new setting, usually outside in the garden, where they would then serve wine, together with many light sweets and small dishes (called *noghl-e mey*) such as fresh or candied dried fruits, nuts, and dragées (nuts coated in sugar). A particular favorite of the sixth-century Persian king Khosrow, who considered it the best dessert and liked to serve it at Nowruz, the Persian New Year, was *lausinaj*. Made of almonds ground together with sugar and rose water in a delicate pastry, it would have been very much like my baklava today. ✑ In this book, I have included a baklava cake and some cookies that are prepared using almond, rice, or chickpea flour, which also makes them gluten- and dairy-free. Try them—they are easy to make and delicious. In the summer, refreshing sharbats are popular in Iran. I have given you my favorite here, made with a vinegar syrup and garnished with cucumber and mint. Teas and infusions are both popular and plentiful in Iran, and I have listed a few that you can make easily, with suggestions for other variations that you might like to try.

FRUIT + NUT CUPCAKES

1 cup (240 ml) olive oil

1 cup (340 g) honey

Zest of 1 orange

¼ cup (60 ml) fresh orange juice

2 tablespoons orange blossom water*

4 eggs (at room temperature)

1 large apple, grated

1 teaspoon baking soda

2 teaspoons baking powder

¼ teaspoon sea salt

1 tablespoon ground cardamom

1½ cups (225 g) white rice flour

1½ cups (145 g) almond flour

DECORATION

¼ cup (30 g) raw, ground pistachio kernels

These are not traditional Yazdi cupcakes, as in my Food of Life *cookbook. Here, I have replaced the flour with almond flour and the yogurt with orange juice, making these light and fluffy in texture and with a lovely fruity flavor. Combining almonds, apples, and honey goes back at least several thousand years in Persian cooking.*

1. Preheat the oven to 350°F (180°C). Line 2 muffin pans (capable of holding 12 muffins each) with paper cups.

2. In a large mixing bowl, combine the oil, honey, orange zest and juice, and orange blossom water, and beat for 1 minute. Add the eggs one by one. Add the grated apple and continue to beat until creamy.

3. Whisk together the baking soda, baking powder, salt, cardamom, rice and almond flours, and gradually add it to the egg mixture. Using a rubber spatula, fold until you have a thick batter.

4. Pour the batter into the paper-lined molds, leaving a ¼ in (5 mm) gap at the top of each cup. Decorate with the pistachios.

5. Place the pan on the center rack in the oven and bake for 25 to 30 minutes, or until a tester inserted into one cupcake comes out clean. Remove the pan from the oven and allow to cool on a cooling rack. Remove the cupcakes from the pan and allow to cool completely on the rack.

6. When ready to serve, arrange the cupcakes on a footed cake dish. Or, you can store in airtight glass containers for up to a week. *Nush-e joon!*

CAKE VARIATION

This batter will also make an excellent cake: Butter an 8in (20cm) round spring-form cake pan and line the base with parchment paper. Butter the parchment paper and dust it with flour. Gently pour the batter into the cake pan and bake in the oven, preheated to 350°F (180°C), for 35 to 40 minutes, or until a tester comes out clean.

FRUIT + NUT CUPCAKES

cayk-e yazdi

CARDAMOM RICE COOKIES

nan-e berenji

Makes 36 cookies
Prep: 20 minutes, plus 30
  minutes for the dough
  to rest
Cooking: 25 minutes

CARDAMOM RICE COOKIES

DOUGH
1 cup olive oil
1½ cups (200 g)
   confectioner's sugar
½ cup (120 ml) rose water*
4 egg yolks
3 cups (450 g) rice flour
   whisked with 1 tablespoon
   ground cardamom,
   1/8 teaspoon fine sea salt,
   and 1 teaspoon poppy
   seeds

DECORATION
2 tablespoons poppy seeds

1. In a mixing bowl, combine the oil, confectioner's sugar, rose water, and egg yolks, and beat until creamy.

2. Add the rice flour mixture and fold until you have a soft dough. Cover and allow the dough to rest for at least 30 minutes in the fridge.

3. Preheat the oven to 300°F (150°C) and line 3 sheet pans with parchment paper or silicone baking mats.

4. Scoop up about 1 tablespoon of the dough (I use an ice-cream scoop) and drop it on one of the lined sheet pans. Repeat with the rest of the dough, leaving 2½ in (6 cm) between each cookie to allow for expansion. Use an offset spatula to lightly flatten each one.

5. Decorate the tops with poppy seeds. Place one sheet of cookies on the center rack in the oven and bake for 20 to 25 minutes, or until the bases show a little color. Keep in mind that the cookies should be white when they are done.

6. Remove the cookies from the oven and allow to cool on a cooling rack while you cook the other batches. When a batch of cookies has cooled, very carefully (as they crumble easily) lift each batch of cookies off the parchment paper using an offset spatula and either serve or store.

7. To store, place the cookies in an airtight glass container and store in the fridge or freezer for up to 3 weeks. *Nush-e joon!*

PISTACHIO COOKIES
nun-e pestehi

Makes 24 cookies
Prep: 5 minutes
Cooking: 10 to 12 minutes

4 cups (500 g) slivered
   pistachio kernels (see note)
2 egg whites
1 cup (130 g) confectioner's
   sugar
⅛ teaspoon sea salt
3 tablespoons rose water*
2 teaspoons ground
   cardamom

NOTE

Slivered pistachios are
available at Iranian markets.
Or, use a food processor to
pulse 4 cups of pistachio
kernels until you have
coarsely chopped pistachios.

Makes: 4
Prep: 10 minutes
Cooking: 20 minutes

GLAZE
½ teaspoon vanilla
¼ cup grape molasses

4 large, firm peaches, halved

GARNISH
1 cup walnut or pecan halves
2 tablespoons grape molasses

PISTACHIO COOKIES

1. Preheat the oven to 350°F (180°C) and line 3 sheet pans with parchment paper.

2. Place all the ingredients in a large mixing bowl and use a rubber spatula to gently mix together until the sugar dissolves (do not over-mix).

3. Scoop up about 1½ tablespoons of the dough (you can use an ice-cream scoop) and drop it on one of the lined sheet pans. Repeat with the rest of the dough, leaving 2½ in (6 cm) between each cookie to allow for expansion.

4. Use an offset spatula, moistened with water, to lightly press down on each cookie to flatten it.

5. Bake on the center rack of the oven for 10 to 12 minutes, or until the cookies are lightly golden around the edges.

6. Remove the sheet pan from the oven and leave to cool on a cooling rack. Remove the cookies from the parchment paper using an offset spatula and store in an airtight glass container for up to 2 weeks. *Nush-e joon!*

ROASTED PEACHES

1. Preheat the oven to 450°F (230°C) and line a sheet pan with parchment paper.

2. In a small bowl, combine the vanilla and grape molasses for the glaze.

3. Arrange the peach halves, cut side up and drizzle the glaze over them. Bake in the oven for 15 to 20 minutes, until peaches are tender.

4. To make the garnish: Toast the walnuts in a wide skillet over medium heat for 5 to 10 minutes shaking the skillet. Add the grape molasses and shake and swirl skillet until all the nuts are covered.

5. To serve, transfer the roasted peaches to a serving platter and garnish with the caramelized walnuts. *Nush-e joon!*

Makes 40 pieces
Prep: 15 minutes plus
  30 minutes resting time
Cooking: 30 minutes

CHICKPEA COOKIES

1 cup (230 ml) olive oil
1 cup (115g) powdered sugar
4 teaspoons ground
  cardamom
1 tablespoon rose water*
3¾ cups (375 g) fine roasted
  chickpea flour, twice sifted
  with ¼ cup unbleached
  all-purpose wheat flour

DECORATION
3 tablespoons slivered raw
  pistachios

NOTE
Fine roasted chickpea flour
and slivered pistachios
are available from Iranian
markets and through the
Internet.

1. In the mixing bowl of an electric mixer, combine oil, sugar, cardamom, and rose water, and mix for 2 to 3 minutes until creamy. Add 3¾ cups chickpea flour and ¼ cup wheat flour mixture, and mix until you have a soft dough (do not over mix).

2. Line a sheet pan with a baking mat or parchment paper and dust it with chickpea flour. Place the dough on top and use your hands to flatten and shape it into a ½-inch-thick square.

3. Cover the entire baking sheet with plastic wrap and use a rolling pin, gently, to even out the dough. Allow to rest at room temperature for 30 minutes at room (or up to 24 hours in the fridge, or place flat in the freezer for up to 3 weeks).

4. Line 2 baking sheets with baking mats or parchment paper. Place the oven rack in the center and preheat the oven to 300°F (150°C).

5. Unwrap the dough. Use a cloverleaf cookie cutter dipped in chickpea flour to cut out the dough. Place cookies on the lined baking sheets, leaving 1 inch between pieces. Decorate each cookie with slivered pistachios.

6. Bake for 30 minutes. Remove baking sheet from oven and place on a cooling rack. When cookies have thoroughly cooled, carefully lift using an offset spatula (be careful, these cookies crumble very easily). Arrange the cookies on a platter. *Nush-e Joon!*

VEGAN

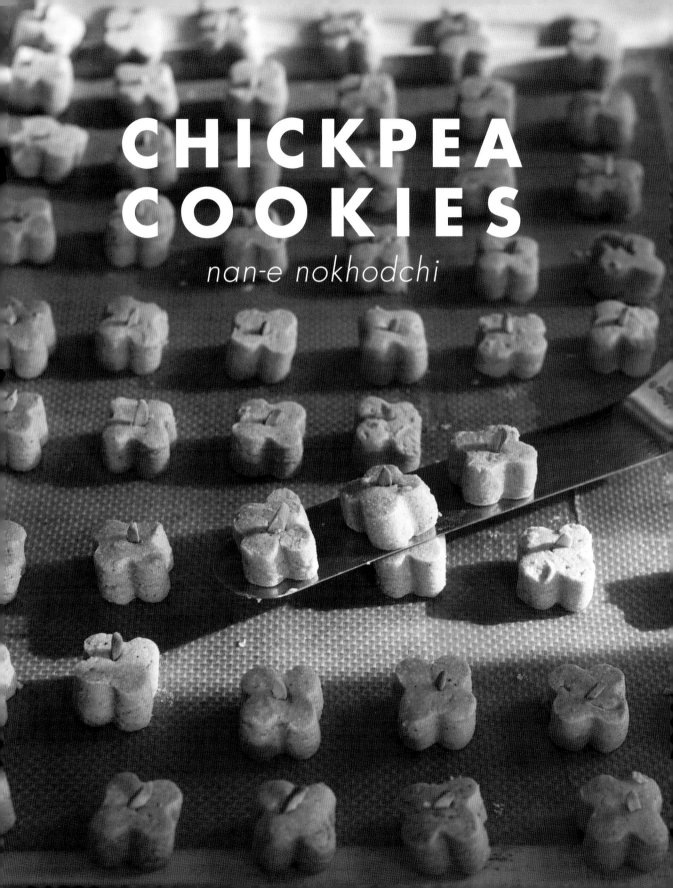

CHICKPEA COOKIES

nan-e nokhodchi

BAKLAVA CAKE

cayk-e baqlava

Makes one 9 x 13in (23 x 33cm)
  sheet pan
Prep: 20 minutes
Cooking: 40 minutes

BAKLAVA CAKE

GLAZE
1 cup (340 g) honey
¼ cup (60 ml) rose water*
Zest of 1 orange
1 tablespoon orange blossom
  water
3 tablespoons fresh lime
  juice

CAKE
3 eggs
¼ cup (85 g) honey
2 tablespoons rose water*
½ cup (120 ml) fresh
  orange juice or milk
½ cup (120 ml) olive oil
1 cup (100 g) unbleached
  all-purpose flour sifted
  with 2 teaspoons baking
  powder
2 cups (190 g) almond meal/
  flour
1 tablespoon ground
  cardamom
2 large, firm applse, peeled,
  cored, and chopped

DECORATION
1 tablespoon chopped raw
  pistachio kernels
1 tablespoon chopped
  blanched almonds

Baklava in the form of a cake, rather than a pastry, is less time-consuming to make and equally delicious. Almonds and apples are a classic combination that is much used in Persian baking. For a gluten-free version of the cake, simply substitute the all-purpose flour with rice flour.

1. In a small saucepan, combine all the ingredients for the glaze. Bring to a boil, reduce heat to low, give the mixture a stir, and simmer for 3 minutes (do not over cook). Remove from heat and set aside.

2. Preheat the oven to 350°F (180°C) and oil a *quarter-sized (9½ x 13 in/ 24 x 33 cm) rimmed sheet pan*.

3. In a mixing bowl, whisk the eggs and honey until creamy. Add the rose water, orange juice, and oil, and whisk for 1 minute longer.

4. Add the flour and baking powder mixture, almond flour, cardamom, and apple, and fold using a rubber spatula.

5. Gently pour the batter into the prepared sheet pan and bake for 35 to 40 minutes, or until a tester comes out clean.

6. Remove the pan from the oven and place it on a cooling rack. Cut the cake into diamond shapes, drizzle the glaze evenly over the hot cake, and decorate with nuts.

7. Leave the cake in the pan until it has absorbed all the glaze and has cooled down completely. Serve from the same pan or transfer to a serving dish.

8. To store and keep moist, wrap tightly with a few layers of clear plastic wrap and store in the fridge for up to 3 weeks. *Nush-e joon!*

Makes one 13 x 18in
 (33 x 45cm) sheet pan
Prep: 10 minutes
Cooking: 15 minutes, plus
 cooling for 30 minutes

SESAME BRITTLE

½ cup (170 g) honey
2 tablespoons rose water*
1½ cups (240 g) hulled
 natural or raw sesame
 seeds
½ teaspoon ground
 cinnamon
½ teaspoon ground nutmeg

This type of brittle—made with sugar, honey, and various nuts and seeds, such as pistachios, almonds, and sesame—has been popular throughout the Middle East since ancient times. In Iran, it is called sohan asali *(honey crunch) or* mama jim jim; *and in Afghanistan, it is known as* hasteh-ye shirin *(sweet kernel). In Masuleh, by the Caspian, I recently tasted several varieties of cookies, all made from sesame seeds.*

1. Line a rimmed sheet pan with a silicone baking mat or parchment paper.

2. Place all the ingredients in a large, deep skillet and use a long-handled wooden spoon to combine and mix well.

3. Cook over medium heat, stirring occasionally, for 10 to 15 minutes, or until golden brown and caramelized.

4. Pour the hot mixture onto the lined sheet pan and immediately flatten and smooth out using an oiled offset spatula.

5. Allow to cool completely (at least 30 minutes) before breaking into pieces and storing in an airtight glass container for up to 3 weeks. *Nush-e joon!*

SESAME BRITTLE

mama jim jim

POMEGRANATE GRANITA

faludeh-ye anar

Serves 6
Prep: 15 minutes, plus freezing
for 4 hours

POMEGRANATE GRANITA

4 cups (950 ml) bottled pure pomegranate juice, or the juice of 8 medium-sized fresh pomegranates

1 cup (340g) ready-made pomegranate syrup

1 tablespoons fresh lime juice

DECORATION

1 cup (150 g) pomegranate arils (about 2 pomegranates)

NOTE

You can use an ice cream machine if you have one. In step 2, pour the mixture into the machine's container and follow the instructions for the machine.

Persian Sharbats, from which we got sherbets, sorbets, granitas, and the now popular drinks called shrubs, could be either sweet or savory. Jean Chardin, traveling in Iran in the seventeenth century, described a favorite of the Isfahanis: sugar, a pinch of salt, pomegranate juice, and a squeeze of garlic and lime, all mixed with crushed ice. This sweet-sour mixture, he found, not only quenched the thirst but stimulated the appetite. Such cool drinks traveled along the trade routes to become the sharbats of Turkey and Syria, the sorbete of Spain, the sorbeto of Italy, the sorbet of France, and the sherbet of England. The European versions were iced mixtures, usually based on fruit, that one ate with a spoon—merely a difference in the degree of freezing. Such frozen desserts in Iran are made with lime juice, sour cherries, or black mulberries and served with sweet rice vermicelli. They have their own name: paludeh or faludeh. A Persian sharbat remains a fruit drink with plenty of ice, often perfumed with rose water or orange blossoms and served in summer in most cities in Iran (see page 208 for one of my favorites).

1. In a wide, shallow container, combine the pomegranate juice, pomegranate syrup, and lime juice, and stir well to mix thoroughly.

2. Place the container, uncovered, in the freezer.

3. Freeze for 2 hours. Break up the frozen juice with a fork and return to the freezer for another hour. Repeat this one more time, or until it becomes like coarsely crushed ice.

4. To serve, use a spoon to scrape up the granita and place in individual serving bowls or glasses. Decorate with the pomegranate arils.

Nush-e joon!

Makes 1 pint (475 ml)
Prep: 10 minutes
Cooking: 30 minutes

VINEGAR + MINT SHARBAT

SYRUP
6 cups (1.2 kg) granulated
  sugar
2 cups (475 ml) water
1½ cups (350 ml) wine
  vinegar
4 sprigs fresh mint

DRINK
Crushed ice
1 cucumber, peeled and
  thinly sliced
2 limes, sliced
1 cup (85 g) fresh mint leaves
½ cup (43 g) fresh cilantro
  leaves
2 tablespoons dried rose
  petals* or marigold
  flowers

The basis for sharbat was the ice and snow that ancient Iranians had learned to preserve during the hot summer months in spectacular domed ice wells on the edges of towns and along caravan routes. The flavorings were syrups, made by combining fruit or vegetable juice with honey, sugar, or date or grape molasses and boiling the mixture down to intensify the flavor. Sipped through a mound of crushed ice or snow, the syrup became a delightful drink. This one, made with vinegar syrup flavored with aromatic herbs, and garnished with lime and cucumbers, is one of my favorites.

1. To make the syrup: Bring the sugar and water to a boil in a medium-sized laminated pot. Simmer over medium heat, stirring occasionally, for 10 minutes, or until the sugar has completely dissolved.

2. Add the vinegar and boil over medium heat for 15 to 20 minutes, or until a thick syrup forms. Add the mint sprigs.

3. Remove from heat and allow to cool. Discard the mint and pour the syrup into a clean, dry bottle. Seal tightly with a cork or screw cap.

4. To make the drink: In a pitcher, mix 1 part syrup with 3 parts water and stir well. Fill half a glass with crushed ice, slices of cucumber, a slice of lime, a few mint and cilantro leaves, and a dried rose petal. Top up the glass with the diluted syrup from the pitcher. *Nush-e joon!*

VINEGAR + MINT SHARBAT

sharbat-e sekanjebin

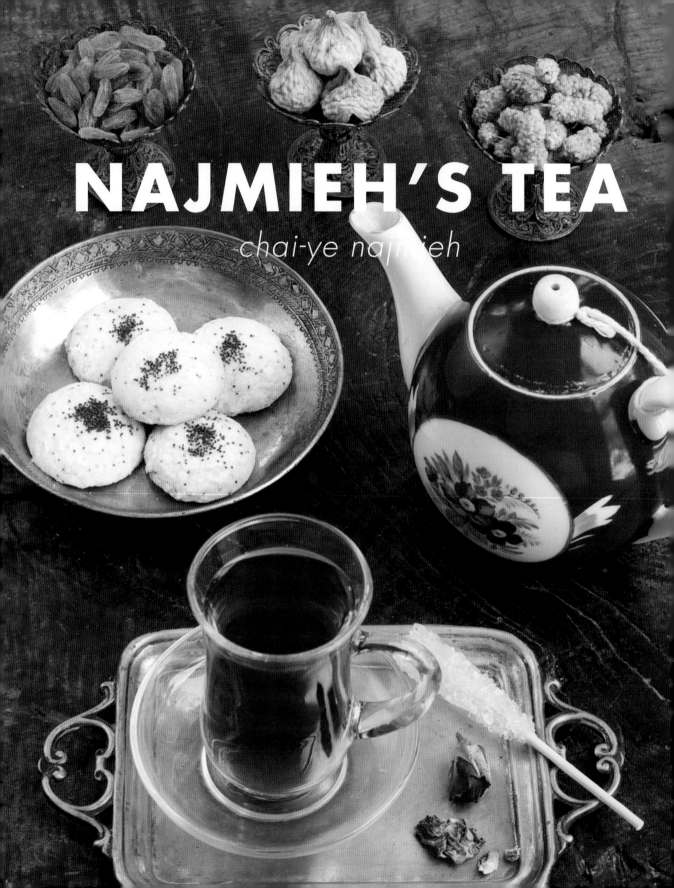

NAJMIEH'S TEA

chai-ye najmieh

Serves 6/Makes one medium-
sized pot

2 tablespoons black tea
   leaves (see note)
1 teaspoon orange blossom
   water*
3 cups (700 ml) boiling water

NOTE

Use an aromatic Persian
blend of black tea leaves,
if possible, available from
Iranian markets: blue/black
labeled Do Ghazal Earl Grey
tea. The orange blossom
water adds a delightful
flavor and aroma.

NAJMIEH'S TEA

Iranians were coffee drinkers from the sixteenth century, but, since taking up tea in the 19th century, they have turned tea making into an art form. A cup of tea must please all the senses. Its color—light red rather than dark brown—should be appreciated, hence it is served in a small glass and not a china cup. It should be steeped for just the right length of time, neither too little nor too long. The temperature and smell are also important: it must be hot and with a heavenly aroma. Tea is offered almost everywhere and without question, as a sign of hospitality, and it's invariably good. If you go to someone's office and they don't offer you a hot glass of tea, you get the message. When I was in Iran last summer, it was the tea that I looked forward to the most.

1. Bring water to a boil in a samovar or tea kettle. Warm a teapot by swirling some boiling water in it and then pour it out. Place the tea leaves and orange blossom water in the pot.

2. Fill the teapot with the 3 cups (700 ml) of boiling water. Replace the lid, cover the pot with a cozy, and let the tea steep for 10 minutes— don't steep for any longer than this as the quality will deteriorate. If you are using a samovar, steep the tea on top.

3. Pour out a glassful of tea and return it to the pot to make sure the tea is evenly mixed.

4. Fill each glass or cup up to halfway with tea, using a tea strainer if you like. Add boiling water from the kettle to dilute the tea to the desired color and taste: some prefer their tea weak, others strong. Keep the pot covered with the cozy while you drink the first glasses. Persian-style tea should always be served good and hot. Refill the glasses frequently (until you've had enough of company and it's time for your guests to leave—I love this kind of subtle sign language). *Nush-e joon!*

INFUSIONS

jushidaniha

The following infusions each make 4 glasses/cups. In each case, boil 4 cups (950 ml) water in a medium-sized saucepan. Add the ingredients, reduce heat to low, cover, and leave to infuse for 15 to 30 minutes. Pour into a teapot and serve in tea glasses or cups, using a tea strainer if you like.

PERSIAN SAFFRON "LOVE" TEA

Saffron tea is traditionally served in parts of Iran to the suitors of the bride as a subtle way of saying yes. Iranians like to use metaphors and sign language, and I love how food is also used as a means of communication.

To the boiling water add 2 cardamom pods, ½ teaspoon ground saffron, 1 tablespoon rose water,* and 2 teaspoons brown sugar. Simmer for 15 minutes.

ROSE PETAL TEA

To the boiling water add 1 clove, 3 cardamom pods, 1 tablespoon dried rose petals,* and 1 teaspoon brown sugar or honey. Simmer for 20 minutes.

BORAGE + VALERIAN NIGHTCAP

To the boiling water add 2 dried limes* (each pierced in several places with the point of a knife), 4 x 1 in (2.5 cm) valerian roots, 2 tablespoons dried borage petals, and 1 teaspoon brown sugar. Simmer for 20 minutes.

JUJUBE PANACEA TEA

Made with jujubes (dried Chinese dates), this tea is particularly popular in Iran and China. My mother would give it to my sisters and me as a panacea, and first line of defense, the moment we complained of some ailment. And there were plenty of other types of herbal tea (*jushundeh*), each for a different complaint.

To the boiling water add ½ cup (75 g) jujubes and simmer for 30 minutes.

GINGER TEA

To the boiling water add grated fresh ginger from a 2 in (5 cm) root, and a squeeze of lime. Simmer for 30 minutes.

OTHER INFUSIONS

Following the instructions above, you can add to the boiling water 2 tablespoons of any of the following: mint, sage, or lemon verbena leaves; thyme sprigs; jasmine, tamarind, or linden flowers; orange blossoms; wild violets; Romaine lettuce leaves; lavender flower heads; dried barberries;* pomegranate arils; fresh or dried sour cherries (unpitted); Seville orange pips; or quince seeds. Depending on your taste, you can add honey or a squeeze of lime. *Nush-e joon!*

QUICK + EASY PERSIAN CUCUMBER PICKLE

khiar shur

Makes: 1 mason jar
Prep: 20 minutes

1 pound (450g) Persian cucumbers , about 6, rinsed
    and thoroughly patted dry. Sliced length-wise
    into quarters
6 cloves garlic, peeled
sprigs of fresh thyme, parsley and dill
2 teaspoons coriander seeds

BRINE
1¾ cups water
1 tablespoon fine sea salt
1 teaspoon sugar

¼ cup apple cider vinegar

1. In a clean mason jar, alternately arrange
the cucumbers, garlic, thyme, parsley, dill, and
coriander seeds.

2. *For the brine:* In a small saucepan, place water,
salt, and sugar, and bring to a boil. Stir well until
salt and sugar are dissolved completely.

3. Fill the jar with the hot brine. Add the vinegar
on top. Close tightly, turn upside down and allow
to sit for 10 to 15 minutes until cool.

    Keep in the fridge for at least 24 hours before
serving. *Nush-e joon!*

TOOLS FOR A PERSIAN KITCHEN

CLEAVER: Instead of a standard chef's knife, I prefer to use an 8 in (20 cm), Japanese-style cleaver. There are a lot of vegetables and herbs to slice and chop in Persian cooking, and this is perfect for the task.

PARING KNIFE: It's useful to have a couple of these.

LONG SERRATED KNIFE: A 5½ in (14 cm) tomato knife is not only good for cutting tomatoes, I find, but bread and melons too.

SKEWERS FOR KABABS: I use two sizes, ½in (1 cm) wide for ground meats, chicken, and sweet and sour kababs, and ¾ in (2 cm) skewers for lamb rib chops.

POTS, PANS, + OVENWARE

ANODIZED POT FOR RICE: For the ultimate Persian rice with a good crust (tah dig), I use a 5-quart (4.7-liter) pot (11¼in/28.5 cm in diameter and 3¼ in/8 cm deep). The best are hard-anodized and non-stick, made by Anolon. They are available at kitchen equipment stores, Iranian markets, or via the Internet.

HEAVY-BOTTOMED POT: I like the Le Creuset enameled cast-iron pots, known in America as Dutch ovens, in England as casserole dishes, and in France as *cocottes*. I use a 2¾-quart (2.6-liter) one for 4 to 6 people. Ideal for slow-cooking and keeping the moisture of braises, they are also great for soups. Natural clay pots—traditionally made in Iran but also produced by potters in America today—are also excellent.

SAUCEPANS WITH LIDS: A small one for making sauces, boiling eggs, and so on, and a medium-sized one for everything else.

LARGE MULTIPOT WITH A LID: This is useful for steaming or boiling vegetables and for boiling pasta. One with a steamer basket is ideal.

LARGE SKILLET WITH A LID: One measuring 12 in (30 cm) across and 2 to 3 in (5 to 8 cm) deep is an essential piece of kitchen equipment.

CAST-IRON SKILLET: One that is 8 to 10in (20 to 25cm) across is particularly useful, such as for making pizza.

RECTANGULAR ROASTING PAN: The standard size is 9 x 13 in (23 x 33 cm). Make sure it's at least 2 to 3 in (5 to 8 cm) deep. This is perfect for roasting of any kind, and especially good for making the meatball recipes in this book.

RIMMED SHEET PAN: At least 2 half-sized (13 x 18 in/33 x 45 cm) ones would be useful. A quarter-sized rimmed sheet pan (9½ x 13 in/24 x 33 cm) is needed for Fresh Herb Kuku and Baklava Cake (pages 104, 200).

KUKU/FRITTATA PAN: Essentially two pans in one, this piece of equipment allows you to cook one side of the kuku/frittata, then flip it over to cook it on the other side.

STAINLESS-STEEL, DEEP, ROUNDED-EDGED SAUTÉ PAN WITH A LID: Useful not only for sautéing but for adding liquid and simmering as well.

KITCHEN TOOLS

MIXING BOWLS & A GOOD WHISK: It's useful to have a selection of stainless-steel mixing bowls in various sizes. A very large one is ideal for washing herbs and much else. Make sure to get a whisk with stainless-steel wires and dishwasher safe.

CUTTING BOARDS: You'll need one for vegetables and another for meat—I prefer to keep them separate. I like to use large cutting boards, preferably made from a single block of wood. If you can afford it, get a Japanese white cypress (hinoki) cutting board. They are medium soft—more likely to keep the edge on your knives—and naturally anti-bacterial.

SPOONS & SPATULAS: For mixing and transferring food, you'll need spoons and spatulas of various sizes, including at least 1 long-handled wooden spoon, a flexible stainless-steel spatula and a silicone one, a ladle, and a spider, which I prefer to a slotted spoon—it's a great tool for poaching eggs and removing vegetables from the pot.

MANDOLIN, MICROPLANE GRATER/ZESTER, & VEGETABLE PEELER: I use a mandolin constantly: it slices in 3 levels of thickness—perfect for cutting up cucumbers, radishes, and apples. Buy the simplest and least expensive one, but take care to not cut your fingers ("no-cry" gloves are available). The microplane is also a must for any kitchen—for grating garlic and ginger, and for removing orange and lemon zest.

ICE-CREAM SCOOP: I use a 2 in (5 cm) one for scooping up equal quantities of paste for meatballs or dough for cookies, as well as for ice cream, of course.

LIME/LEMON SQUEEZER: I find that I use lime juice more and more in my cooking. This tool is wonderful for squeezing the juice from lemons or limes as it gets every drop.

TONGS: It's best to avoid tongs with locks on them because they can lock of their own accord when you are using them. Also, shorter ones are more functional than long ones.

MITTS & DISH TOWELS: I recommend silicone mitts as they last longer than cloth ones. Every kitchen should have a good set of large dish towels. You'll need a clean one for tying around the lid of your rice pot, for instance, to seal it so that the steam can't escape.

MEASURING CUPS, SPOONS, & WEIGHING SCALE: A 2-cup (1-pint/475 ml) measuring cup is useful, and you will need a set of smaller measuring cups and spoons, together with a scale for weighing certain ingredients.

TIMERS: I like to keep mine simple, but the basic clockwork kind that you wind up is harder to find these days. Make sure you have one that continues to count after it has rung, which can be useful if you didn't hear it go off. Mobile phones also have a very useful timer function.

COLANDERS & STRAINERS: A wide fine-mesh colander is excellent for quickly draining rice, good inexpensive ones are available at Iranian and Chinese markets. Recently, I found a white plastic Japanese strainer on the Internet. Made with narrow slits, it's specifically designed for draining rice after washing it.

SALAD SPINNER: A stainless-steel spinner will last longer. Besides drying lettuce with one, I also use it for soaking, washing, and drying herbs.

SHEET-PAN LINER/BAKING MAT: You can always use parchment paper for lining sheet pans, but silicone baking mats and sheet-pan liners are ideal for baking Persian cookies, and more economical as they can be reused.

PARCHMENT PAPER: Rolls and pre-cut sheets of parchment paper are useful, not only for lining sheet pans, but also for covering food in the oven, where the paper provides a non-reactive layer between the food and outer covering of aluminum foil. Parchment paper is not the same as waxed paper and therefore should not be substituted for it.

KITCHEN APPLIANCES

FOOD PROCESSOR: An essential time saver in the kitchen these days. My preferred one is a 14-cup Kitchen Aid. I use it for grinding nuts, and chopping onions and vegetables. It is especially good for chopping up herbs.

RICE COOKER: A 3-cup (700 ml) rice cooker is a very useful piece of equipment. Be sure to use a standard measuring cup for the measurements that I give in the recipes and not the one that might be provided with the rice cooker. Buy the brands available from Iranian markets: their thermostats have been set for making a good rice crust (tah dig). I use a Pars rice cooker it's simple and inexpensive.

SPICE GRINDER: I recommend you always grind spices yourself rather than purchasing ready-ground ones. You can easily taste and smell the difference between black pepper freshly ground in a grinder and the ready-ground variety. This is equally true for other spices, such as saffron, cardamom pods, and cumin seeds (however, for turmeric, the already ground powder is fine).

Najmieh buying
kale at the Fresh
Farms Market.

INDEX

Najmieh Batmanglij was born and raised in Iran. During her childhood, her mother wouldn't allow her in the kitchen. "Concentrate on your education," she would say. "There will be plenty of time for you to cook later in life."

Najmieh came to America in the 1960s to study at university and would cook Persian food with fresh local produce using recipes sent by her mother in letters. Her housemates loved the food she made and encouraged her to cook all the more. Little did she know that the American food revolution had just begun. Later, when Najmieh returned to Iran with her master's degree in education in hand, her mother welcomed her into the kitchen and started to work with her.

At the end of 1979, as the Iranian Revolution took a more fundamentalist turn, Najmieh and her husband fled to France, where their first son Zal was born.